2005

THE BEST 10-MINUTE PLAYS
FOR THREE OR MORE ACTORS

D1526962

Smith and Kraus'
Short Plays and 10-Minute Plays Collections

Christopher Durang Vol. I: 27 Short Plays

Frank D. Gilroy Vol. II: 15 One-Act Plays

Israel Horovitz Vol. I: 16 Short Plays

Romulus Linney 17 Short Plays

Terrence McNally Vol. I: 15 Short Plays

Lanford Wilson: 21 Short Plays

Act One Festival 1995: The Complete One-Act Plays

Act One Festival 1994: The Complete One-Act Plays

EST Marathon 1999: The Complete One-Act Plays

EST Marathon 1998: The Complete One-Act Plays

EST Marathon 1997: The Complete One-Act Plays

EST Marathon 1996: The Complete One-Act Plays

EST Marathon 1995: The Complete One-Act Plays

EST Marathon 1994: The Complete One-Act Plays

HB Playwrights Short Play Festival

    2003 The Subway Plays

    2002 The Beach Plays

    2001 The Hospital Plays

    2000 The Funeral Plays

    1999 The Airport Plays

    1998 The Museum Plays

    1997 The Motel Plays

Twenty One-Acts from 20 Years at the Humana Festival 1975–1995

The Women's Project and Productions Rowing to America and Sixteen Other Short Plays

8 TENS @ 8 Festival: 30 10-Minute Plays from the Santa Cruz Festivals I–VI

30 Ten-Minute Plays from the Actors Theatre of Louisville for 2 Actors

30 Ten-Minute Plays from the Actors Theatre of Louisville for 3 Actors

30 Ten-Minute Plays from the Actors Theatre of Louisville for 4, 5, and 6 Actors

2004: The Best 10-Minute Plays for Two Actors

2004: The Best 10-Minute Plays for Three or More Actors

2005
THE BEST 10-MINUTE PLAYS
FOR THREE OR MORE
ACTORS

Edited by D. L. Lepidus

CONTEMPORARY PLAYWRIGHT SERIES

A Smith and Kraus Book
Hanover, New Hampshire

Published by Smith and Kraus, Inc.
177 Lyme Road, Hanover, NH 03755
www.SmithandKraus.com
(888) 282-2881

First Edition: August 2007
10 9 8 7 6 5 4 3 2 1

Manufactured in the United States of America
Cover and Text Design by Julia Hill Gignoux, Freedom Hill Design
Cover photo by Gen Hasagawa: Eleanor Janecek Delaney, Krista Schwarting, and Jeff McCamish in the Kokopelli Theatre Company production at the Last Frontier Theatre Conference of *An Ongoing Examination of the True Meaning of LIfe* by S. W. Senek.

ISBN-10 1-57525-530-8
ISBN-13 978-1-57525-530-9
ISSN 1550-6754
Library of Congress Control Number: 2007930047

Contents

INTRODUCTION *by D. L. Lepidus*   vii

PLAYS FOR 3 ACTORS

Shot Americans (3W) by Kayla Cagan 3

Larry Gets the Call (2W, 1M) by Matt Casarino 11

Shades (1W, 2M) by Mark Harvey Levine 19

Every Man (2W, 1M) by Michael Niederman. 27

Molly Whuppie (2W, 1M) by Don Nigro 35

It's Called Development (3W) by Anne Phelan. 41

An Ongoing Examination of the True Meaning of Life
   (2W, 1M or 1W, 2M) by S. W. Senek. 47

Pistachio Stories (2W, 1M) by Laura Shamas. 59

The Searcher (1W, 2M) by Frederick Stroppel. 65

More (1W, 2M) by Jeff Tabnick 75

Weird Water (1W, 2M) by Robert Lewis Vaughan. 83

Dead Boy (2W, 1M) by Craig Wright 93

PLAYS FOR 4 ACTORS

Vinny's Vision (4M) by Jim Gordon 107

Betting the Karmic House (1W, 3M or 2W, 2M) by Bill Johnson . . 115

Infant Morality (3W, 1M) by Craig Pospisil 123

How to Speak Man (4M) by Sharyn Rothstein 131

Remind Me Again (3W, 1M) by Sharyn Rothstein 143

Hell Hath Three Furies (3W, 1M) by Aoise Stratford. 151

A Moment of Your Undivided Attention (3W, 1M)
   by Alina Trowbridge 159

PLAYS FOR 5 ACTORS

Tina at the Times *or Below the Fold* (2W, 3M) by Wendy MacLeod. . . 167

PLAYS FOR 6 OR MORE ACTORS

Toys in Babeland (1W, 8M) by Delilah Gomez. 175

at the time (5W, 3M) by Winter Miller. 181

Small World (3W, 3M) by Tracey Scott Wilson 189

PERMISSION ACKNOWLEDGMENTS 198

Introduction

The ten-minute play as an accepted dramatic form is a fairly recent development. Some would say that its popularity is a result of our diminished attention spans, which may be partially true. But here's how the genre came to be.

For several years, Actors Theatre of Louisville, under the leadership of Jon Jory, commissioned playwrights to write plays of short duration for performance by its apprentice company. This was a way for the theater to do something to help playwrights, but also it was a way to develop relationships with them, many of which bore fruit over the years as these writers went on to have full-length plays staged in Actors Theatre's famed Humana Festival.

Over the years, Actors Theatre built up quite a library of these short plays, all of them in manuscript. The play publisher Samuel French got the idea that maybe other theaters, actors, and students might be interested in these plays if they were made available to them. They managed to swing a deal to publish an anthology of Actors Theatre's best short plays, which they were now calling "ten-minute plays." This anthology was so successful that French has now published six such volumes, and most of the other publishers have followed suit, including Smith and Kraus, as its annual ten-minute plays anthologies will attest. Bills of ten-minute plays are now produced regularly, all over the world.

There are some who feel that the ten-minute play ought to be an opportunity for playwrights to experiment — with language, with form, with character, with subject matter. "The best" ten-minute plays are therefore the ones that depart the most from conventional drama. For the purposes of this series, I define *best* as: that which is most useful to people who will buy this book and produce these plays. Hard as it may be for dramaturges and such-like to imagine, not everybody cares for plays that seek to reinvent the dramatic form. Directors like the more experimental-type play, though, which gives them a better opportunity to call attention to their work than the more conventional, or realistic, play, which generally requires direction that is more or less invisible. I have therefore included some plays in a less conventional style that I hope will appeal to directors as well as to actors who like this kind of play.

Should you find a play (or plays) in this book that you want to produce, you will find information in the back on who to contact for performance rights.

D. L. Lepidus
Brooklyn, N.Y.

PLAYS FOR
THREE ACTORS

Shot Americans

K AYLA C AGAN

CHARACTERS
SCOTTY SCOTLAND: (AKA SCOZZY), the older sister of Sammy, the leader
of Fallacy, their performance art band; mid-twenties
SAMMY SCOTLAND: the younger sister of Scotty, the drummer of Fallacy;
early twenties
DAKOTA BLAND: Fallacy guitarist and friend of Sammy and Scotty, early
twenties

SETTING
Taos, New Mexico. One of the many apartments they have inherited from
their father. It is now decorated with Scotty and Sammy's trashed-out,
want-to-be-rock-star style.

TIME
Now

•   •   •

*It is noon. Scotty, Sammy, and Dakota sit in a trashed-out apartment in Taos,
New Mexico. They obviously have money, but they are young and reckless, and
cleanliness sucks. Sammy is smoking a joint, Dakota strums on her guitar,
Scotty reads the newspaper. They are all bleary-eyed.*

SAMMY: *(Slowly.)* I'm gonna make breakfast.
DAKOTA: OK.
SAMMY: Anyone want?
DAKOTA: Yeah.
SAMMY: What?
DAKOTA: Huh?
SAMMY: What do you want, man?
DAKOTA: Ummm. Eggs.
SAMMY: OK. How?
DAKOTA: Fried. And delicious.
SAMMY: Nope.
DAKOTA: OK. Just fried.
SAMMY: *(Sings.)* FRIED?
DAKOTA: *(Sings back.)* FRIED!
SAMMY: What do you want, Scoz?
    (Scotty doesn't respond.)
SAMMY: What do you want to eat, Scozzy?

SCOTTY: Huh?

SAMMY: You've got to eat.

SCOTTY: Yeah. OK. What you havin'?

DAKOTA: We're all havin' eggs, man.

SCOTTY: Scramble 'em up, then.

DAKOTA: What are you reading?

SCOTTY: Freakin' paper.

SAMMY: We can see that.

DAKOTA: Any news?

SCOTTY: Yeah. Yep. There's news every day, isn't there?

SAMMY: What's it say now?

SCOTTY: Ah. Degenerates. Assholes.

DAKOTA: America still hates you?

SCOTTY: Hates me?

SAMMY: Hates US! Fuck yeah!

SCOTTY: That wasn't the point.

DAKOTA: Somebody's always gonna be pissed.

SCOTTY: Yeah.

SAMMY: But we can't be pissed right?

SCOTTY: We made Sarah Smith's column again. We haven't even been out of the city for a freakin' day. Check this shit out: "Once again, Dead Celebrity Matthew Peterson Scotland should be turning over in his grave. Scotland, a professional dancer and an immigrant to this country, had always been a quote unquote "American in his heart." Now his two dangerous daughters, Samantha Peterson Scotland and Jennifer "Scotty" Scotland and their cohort Dakota Bland in their art performance band, Fallacy, are at it again with their stage pranks. With their recent show in Soho, they not only came off as unpatriotic, but unpolished and unprofessional as well. I'm no art critic, but if I were you, I'd say FALLACY is a FALLACY. In other news, Rupert Everett announces he will play Richard Chamberlain in the movie *That's Dick to You, Buddy.*

SAMMY: Great. It's exactly what we wanted. Who gives a shit about Sarah Smith? And we are booked in New York for the entire Fall.

DAKOTA: Yeah. It's no big shit.

SCOTTY: Here's the shit. Sarah Smith doesn't know the first thing about our father. How dare she write he should roll over in his grave.

SAMMY: He's proud of us. You know that. I'm gonna start the eggs.

DAKOTA: She's bullshit.

SCOTTY: Well, that bullshit sells. And Dad has a lot more fans than we do.

DAKOTA: So, what are you worried about? Sales? When did we ever think we were going to get rich?

SAMMY: We're rich now, it doesn't matter. Coffee?

SCOTTY: Yeah, we're rich off of Dad busting his ass and breaking his toes and tearing his ligaments.

DAKOTA: He wanted you guys to be taken care of, and he loved to dance. So, if he made money off it, what's wrong with that?

SCOTTY: You guys don't get it.

SAMMY: We're just off a red-eye, we've got jet lag, and you've got a hangover and stink like ass. So, you're readin' a paper that sucks, with a columnist who sucks, and we're at home and we need to eat and sleep. We can talk about it after coffee.

SCOTTY: No. I don't want to talk about it after coffee.

DAKOTA: OK, go. What's your point?

SCOTTY: My point is that fuckin' Sarah Smith writes about Dad like he's a fucking perfect American, or rather "American in his heart" immigrant. But what the hell is that? He got just as many bad reviews when he started off creating his work. And he fled a fucking other country to get here, and landed here with nothing, and then was treated like nothing for the longest time. He drank.

SAMMY: No doubt.

SCOTTY: He smoked.

DAKOTA: Who doesn't?

SCOTTY: He was high all of the time.

SAMMY: Well, so am I —

SCOTTY: But he was miserable. Do you ever remember seeing him happy? His nightmares, his walking trances. I thought he had fuckin' Alzheimer's, but no, it wasn't that. All he could do was dance, his way of running. When we were born, it made him slow down, he dragged us with him. But we made him miserable.

SAMMY: No, we didn't!

SCOTTY: Yes, we did. You were just too young to realize it.

SAMMY: He loved us.

SCOTTY: OK.

SAMMY: You don't think he loved us?

DAKOTA: You guys are crazy. He loved both of you. He just had very particular demons.

SCOTTY: So, now we are disappointing him according to fucking Sarah Smith.

SAMMY: You are just letting some dumb writer get to you. She even says she's not an art critic, she wouldn't know an easel from her ass and she certainly doesn't understand movement, so you know, just drop her.

DAKOTA: No more newspapers for you, Scoz.

SCOTTY: I'm OK. It's just . . .

DAKOTA: What?

SCOTTY: I just can't drop this. I can't drop her and I can't drop him.

SAMMY: But she doesn't count. She's a parasite! She makes her life off of our lives and our friend's life, and even our dead father's life. Don't let her rule you. It will change you. It will change us. It will change what we do and how we do it. No Inteference, Ladies! No interference!

DAKOTA: We create. And what comes out of us, comes out of us.

SAMMY: And if we're funny, we're funny.

DAKOTA: And if we're shallow, we're shallow.

SAMMY: And if we're brilliant, we're brilliant.

DAKOTA: But we do it. We create. Just like your dad did.

SAMMY: I think he would be damn proud of our performance this weekend, Scoz.

SCOTTY: You think so?

SAMMY: I have a feeling.

SCOTTY: You know, if he was "American in his heart," he was also American in the worst kinds of way. He imported all of his shit, his tricks, his conning. The only beautiful thing he did was dance.

DAKOTA: He put a roof over your head. He's no worse than any other American.

SAMMY: I can't tell if you are mad at him or you think he's mad at us.

SCOTTY: How old were you guys when you had your first shot?

DAKOTA: Shot?

SCOTTY: Tequila, whiskey, whatever . . .

SAMMY: Well, you know I was a teenager. I don't know, sixteen or seventeen?

DAKOTA: I was in college, I think.

SCOTTY: I was nine.

DAKOTA: What?

SCOTTY: With Dad.

SAMMY: I never knew that.

SCOTTY: Dad was showing me how to pirouette and I fell, really hard, and scraped myself.

He poured whiskey on my ankle and then we each took a shot.

SAMMY: Wow.

DAKOTA: How did it taste?

SCOTTY: I puked.

(They all laugh.)

SCOTTY: It's not really funny.

SAMMY: Yeah it is.

DAKOTA: That's disgusting, man.

SCOTTY: Yep.

SAMMY: I never knew that.

SCOTTY: I know. There's a lot you never knew about Dad.

DAKOTA: Guess not.

SCOTTY: But it's still in me, you know.

SAMMY: What?

SCOTTY: That first shot.

SAMMY: Oh, I thought you puked it out. *(Dakota and Sammy laugh.)*

SCOTTY: No, it's in me. It's *(She indicates different body parts.)* here and here and here.

   He's never left me. That first drink has never left me. Why do you think I have a shot before I go onstage?

SAMMY: *(Coughing into her hand.)* Al-co-holic!

SCOTTY: So if I fall, if we fall, it won't hurt. It flows in me, it's the burnin' fuel in the veins, it heats me. I can't do shit without it, without him. And then some bitch says we disappoint him. Well, it takes fucking courage to go up in front of people and lay out emotion. It takes blood on fire to tell people the story of their country and your country and the magnificence of history. And it's all twined together, see. She knocks us for doing something that means something to us. Every time we create, it hurts.

DAKOTA: Um —

SAMMY: What?

DAKOTA: I've never felt that.

SCOTTY: It's not in your blood.

DAKOTA: But —

SCOTTY: No, Dak, you're great at what you do, but it's different for Sam and I. It's what happens in sisters, what happens in family. We have the same blood circulating in us. That's why I drink, that's why she smokes.

SAMMY: That's not why I smoke.

SCOTTY: OK.

SAMMY: You don't believe me?

SCOTTY: Why do you smoke?

SAMMY: It's habit.

SCOTTY: Fair enough.

DAKOTA: I feel like I'm missing out.

SCOTTY: You're not.

DAKOTA: Why is that?

SCOTTY: You've got your own sticks and mud. You've got your own family, your own blood, your own country inside of you.

DAKOTA: I always knew there was a reason you were the front woman.

SCOTTY: And you thought it was just passion.

DAKOTA: You're carrying out your father's dream.

SCOTTY: No, not his dream —

SAMMY: — his skin.

SCOTTY: You get it, now.

SAMMY: I'm starting, too.

DAKOTA: Yeah.

SCOTTY: I don't carry anyone's dream, anyone's experience, anyone's failure. I lug habit, movement, gesture, bite. One day, I'll figure out who the hell I am. Until then, he'll run through my veins and out onto the stage.

DAKOTA: He's a ghost inside.

SCOTTY: And he hates the terrain.

SAMMY: We need to eat.

DAKOTA: Yeah, let's chow.

SCOTTY: I think I'll just have a drink instead.

(They both look at Scotty. Sammy goes to the kitchen, pulls out three shot glasses, and pours them each a drink. They tap glasses.)

SAMMY: To Dad

DAKOTA: To Drink

SCOTTY: To the American in his heart!

ALL: Arrrrggggg!!!! *(The cheer they do for their drinks.)*

(They throw back their shots. Each makes a face.)

SAMMY: Yow!

DAKOTA: Too early!

SCOTTY: Still burns.

(Scotty looks at the others, and pours again. This time she lifts her glass, the others don't.)

SCOTTY: To our founding father . . .

(Scotty slams back the drink while the others watch. Lights fade as Scotty continues to slam shots.)

END OF PLAY

Larry Gets the Call

MATT CASARINO

Larry Gets the Call debuted at the Pittsburgh New Works Festival in September, 2005. The cast was as follows: God: Toniaray Digiacomo; Petra: Joanna Lowe; Larry: Everett Lowe. Directed by Joseph A. Roots. Produced by Rage of the Stage Players. *Larry Gets the Call* debuted Off-Off-Broadway with Emerging Artists Theatre in November, 2005. The cast was as follows: God: Christine Bruno; Petra: Rebecca Nyahay; Larry: Ron Bopst. Directed by Melissa Attebery. Produced by Emerging Artists Theatre.

CHARACTERS

GOD: a physically disabled woman. Any age.

PETRA: God's assistant. Affable woman, any age.

LARRY: at least twenty-five. Looks disheveled, like he's been sleeping

The author requests that the role of "God" be played by a physically disabled actress.

SETTING

An office

•   •   •

Scene: An "office," with a couple of nice chairs in a conversation setup. Maybe some plants and pictures on the wall, but nothing fancy. Petra walks in, arm and arm with Larry. She's garrulous and informal; he's a little bewildered.

PETRA: . . . so then the giraffe says "Will you pipe down! If I can hear you from up here you are too loud!" *(She laughs.)* True story. So. Larry. This your first time?

LARRY: My first time what?

PETRA: Your first time here?

LARRY: Um . . . I don't think I know where "here" is.

PETRA: Oh, of course you do, honey. Don't worry. Just have a seat.

LARRY: Am I dreaming?

PETRA: Not quite. It'll be fine. Just take a nice deep breath, have a seat . . .

LARRY: Which one?

PETRA: . . . doesn't matter, just bend those knees . . . that's a good boy. *(Larry sits.)* OK. Well, as usual, we're running a little behind, but don't you worry. God will be here in just a minute. Good luck Larry! *(Exits.)*

LARRY: Thank you. *(A few beats.)* Wait. What? Who will be here?

GOD: *(Offstage.)* Bonjour!

(God enters. God is a disabled woman. She walks over to Larry, gives him a kiss on the head, smiles, and sits in the unoccupied chair.)

GOD: *Bonjour! Bienvenue! Je suis désolé que nous courions tard. Elle se produit toute l'heure. Mais bienvenue! Ainsi, c'est lui. Que pense-tu?*

Hello! Welcome! I'm sorry we're running late. It happens all the time. But welcome! So, this is it. What do you think?

LARRY: What?

(God frowns, and checks her notebook.)

GOD: Monsieur . . . Humpert?

LARRY: Um . . . Larry. I'm Larry.

GOD: LARRY! Geez, I'm sorry Larry. Stupid planner. *(Yelling offstage.)* I told you this planner wouldn't help!

PETRA: *(Offstage.)* It would if you used it properly!

GOD: Anyway. Larry! Hi!

LARRY: Hi.

(Beat.)

GOD: So I'm God.

LARRY: What?

GOD: I'm God. Ta da!

LARRY: But . . .

GOD: It's true. God exists. Come on, you always knew. Remember, back in fourth grade? You fell out of that tree, and you broke your leg, and you asked me not to take you, and I reached down and patted you on the head and said "Don't worry, child." Remember?

LARRY: I never fell out of a tree.

(God checks her planner.)

GOD: Damn it! *(Yelling offstage.)* Petra, this thing's all screwed up again!

PETRA: *(Offstage.)* Look in the left column, God. Remember? Alternate columns for alternate hemispheres?

GOD: *(Yelling offstage.)* I don't know why you think I can handle one of these things. You've seen my work.

PETRA: *(Offstage.)* You promised you'd give it a try.

GOD: Fine. Sorry about that, sweetie. OK. *(Puts down planner.)* You were seven, and you were having your tonsils out. Remember now?

LARRY: Yeah. I remember that.

GOD: Remember when they wheeled you into the operating room, and you were so afraid, and you were trying to be brave and not cry . . .

LARRY: Yeah. Wow, yeah, I remember that. I remember how the gas mask smelled . . . it was so strong, so strange . . .

GOD: So you asked me to help you wake up. Remember? Right before you went to sleep, you asked me to help you wake up. And before you went to sleep, I said . . .

LARRY: "I will."

GOD: Yes! "I will!" You were so small, so scared, but so brave, and . . . oh, great, now I'm crying, hold on . . .

LARRY: You are God!

GOD: I am God! *(Blows nose.)*

LARRY: So you're . . . um . . .

GOD: *(Sighs.)* Yes, Larry. It's a shock, I know. But it's true. I'm a woman.

LARRY: Uh . . .

GOD: Hey, what can I tell ya? All those painters got it wrong. Why do you people keep painting me as an old guy with a beard? Hello! I'm God! I shave! *(Standing.)* Still, not bad, right? Check these out . . . *(Sticks out breasts.)* Booyah! Not too shabby, right? Hey, wanna see how I made the Alps? *(Cups breasts, then shoots them like guns.)* BAM! BAM!

LARRY: No! No, I mean . . . um . . . you . . .

GOD: Yes?

LARRY: You have . . . um . . .

GOD: Nice hair? What?

LARRY: No . . . I mean, yes, your hair is very nice . . .

GOD: You think? *(Sits again.)* I just had it done, but I don't know. I'm not thrilled. Anyway, we could talk about my hair all day, babe. Believe me. But that's not why you're here. *(Beat.)* You want some lemonade?

LARRY: Well, no, I don't . . .

GOD: You sure? Come on, give it a go. It's from God! *(Yelling offstage.)* Petra? Sweetie?

PETRA: *(Offstage.)* Lemonade's coming right up!

GOD: Isn't she fabulous? Love her!

PETRA: *(Offstage.)* Did you tell him yet?

GOD: I'm getting to it now!

PETRA: *(Offstage.)* We're behind schedule.

GOD: I know.

PETRA: *(Offstage.)* Again.

GOD: I know! I'm doing it now, OK? Geez!

LARRY: Wait, I think I get it!

GOD: *(Delighted.)* You do?

LARRY: Yes! Yes! See, you . . . you are just a visual concept of God that I can understand! You're appearing to me like this, in a form that I can process, instead of your true form! Of course!

(Beat.)

GOD: What?

LARRY: You're . . . I mean . . .

GOD: This is me, kiddo. You wanna see it again? *(Cups breasts.)* BAM BAM!

LARRY: So . . . you mean you're really . . .

GOD: Look . . . I would love to chat about me, my true form, the Alps. Really. But Petra's right . . . the schedule is tight, and as I'm constantly reminded, time is short. So I'm going to have to get right to it. *(Sits up, a little more formal.)* Lawrence . . . *(Steals a glance at her notebook.)* Gregory Christopher . . . I hereby appoint thee a prophet of the Lord. *(Beat. Petra enters with the lemonade.)*

PETRA: Here we go!

GOD: Wonderful! Thank you so much. Seriously, babe, try some. It's good.

LARRY: A prophet of the Lord?

GOD: Mmmmhmm.

LARRY: That can't be!

GOD: No, it's true. Right Petra?

PETRA: Right as always.

GOD: Yep. So what do you think?

LARRY: I can't be a prophet!

GOD: Why not?

LARRY: I'm just a guy!

GOD: Well, that's what prophets are. Except when they're gals.

LARRY: But I'm just a guy, a schmo! I . . . I'm not a minister or a rabbi or anything! I work at Borders! I only go to church on Christmas! I write bad
poems, I have dirty DVDs, I have a dog who keeps pooping in the apartment . . .

GOD: I love dogs! What kind?

PETRA: I think he's a little freaked.

GOD: I know. They all are. Weird, huh? Listen. Lenny . . .

PETRA: Larry.

GOD: . . . Larry . . . it's not that big of a deal. Well, I mean it is, you're here
talking to God, and hey, she's a stunner! But it's not like you have to
become a priest or anything.

LARRY: I don't?

GOD: Of course not. Unless you want to. Here's how it works. I have a message for you. And I want you to communicate this message to other people.

LARRY: You mean . . . spread the word?

PETRA: Something like that, yes.

LARRY: Like . . . go on TV and tell everyone I talked to God?

GOD: Ach!

PETRA: Goodness no!

GOD: I asked you to communicate my message, not to be a jerk about it!

LARRY: Then . . . how?

PETRA: Listen, I'll leave you two alone. *(Starts to exit.)* God . . . really . . . *(She
taps her wrist.)*

GOD: I know! Larry . . . I just want you to express the message. However you
want to. In whatever way pleases you. In song. In conversation. In dance.
In the way you smile. It's up to you, baby. *(Beat.)* Are you going to try
my lemonade or not?

LARRY: Oh. I'm sorry. Yes. *(Takes a sip.)* It's good.

GOD: Really? It's not too sweet?

LARRY: No, it's good.

GOD: I was afraid it was too sweet. I like it sweet. *(Yelling offstage.)* He likes the lemonade, Petra!

PETRA: I knew he would!

GOD: So . . . are you ready, Larry? For your message?

LARRY: Well . . . sure. I guess. Yes.

GOD: OK. Here it is. *(Leans in, and talks slowly.)* I am a reflection of the world. And the world is a reflection of me.
   (Beat.)

LARRY: Is that all?

GOD: That's all.

LARRY: I don't get it.

GOD: You don't? Geez, I worked so hard on wording that just right . . . OK, let me try again. Larry. *(Leans in, but this time uses hand gestures while talking.)* I am . . . a . . . reflection . . . of the world. And the world is . . . a . . . reflection . . . of me. See?

LARRY: You are a reflection of the world.

GOD: And the world . . .

LARRY: . . . and the world is a reflection of you.

GOD: Right!

LARRY: *(Beat.)* I think I understand.

GOD: You do?

LARRY: Yeah! Yeah, I really do!

GOD: That's fabulous!

LARRY: Yes! Yes I get it! It all makes sense now! You're saying that we, meaning mankind, have . . . we've tainted the world. It's damaged. We've damaged the world, we've . . . we fight each other, we kill each other . . . we're ruining it. We . . . Oh! We are crippling the world. I get it, God. We've taken this beautiful gift of land, of life, of love, but we've abused it. And now it's damaged. It's crippled. And that's reflected . . . that's reflected in you. We're crippling the world, and as a result . . . we've crippled God. *(Starts to cry.)* We've crippled God! I'm sorry, God, I'm so sorry . . . *(Cries, with his head in his hands.)*
   (God rises. Slowly she walks over to Larry, and puts her hands on his. She gently lifts his head, lowers his hands, and looks into his eyes with deep compassion. And then . . .)
   (She slaps him.)

GOD: No! I meant that the world is pretty, like me!

LARRY: Oh. Um . . .

GOD: "We've crippled God?" What the hell?

LARRY: I'm sorry. I thought . . .

GOD: You do think I'm pretty, right?

LARRY: Yes!

GOD: Or are you one of those . . . you know . . . *(Does the "queer" hand motion.)*

LARRY: What?

GOD: You know what I mean. You know they're abominations, right?

LARRY: *(Wide-eyed.)* They are?

   (Beat. God starts to laugh.)

GOD: No! *(Laughs.)* Gotcha! Aw, listen, I'm sorry I slapped you, sweetie, but
   nobody calls me damaged, and NOBODY calls me crippled. Got it?

LARRY: I'm sorry.

GOD: It's OK. I forget how hard this must be sometimes. Listen, don't be telling
   people I said anyone was an abomination, OK? I was just kidding about
   that.

LARRY: So . . . so they're not?

GOD: Of course not. If one thing should be clear to you people, it's that I like
   a little variety.

LARRY: So . . . so do you want me to spread that message too? That they, you
   know, they're not . . .

GOD: No, don't bother. I've given that message to plenty of prophets already.
   Of course, they all turned out to be playwrights . . . no. You just stick
   with your message, OK? You got a good one.

LARRY: But . . . but I still don't understand . . .

GOD: It's OK. You will. Look at me, sweetie. I know the world is not a perfect place. I know how hard it is for you people. I see what goes on . . .
   but you're better off. Believe me. Perfection is . . . sterile. It's boring. It
   doesn't fit. It's all wrong. That's why I kicked Adam and Eve out of the
   garden.

LARRY: I thought that was because they stole an apple?

GOD: Oh, please! I totally made that up! I still can't believe they fell for it.
   "Hey, you guys ate my special . . . um . . . apple!" *(Laughs.)* Those two,
   I tell ya . . . nice kids, but not my best work, if you know what I mean.
   Ah, well, I was young. Anyway . . . they didn't belong in a perfect world.
   Nobody does, Larry. *(Leans in, gives a sad smile.)* Least of all me. *(Beat.)*
   Are you starting to understand?

LARRY: I . . . I think so . . .

GOD: Give it time. You will. Not too much time, though. OK?

LARRY: OK. So . . .

GOD: So it's time for you to go. *(Yells offstage.)* Petra? We're ready!

LARRY: God?

GOD: Yeah?

LARRY: Can I ask you a question?

GOD: Sure! *(Beat, as Larry says nothing.)* What?

LARRY: *(Struggling.)* I . . . I have so many, I don't . . .

GOD: Shhhh.

> *(Petra enters.)*

GOD: *(Continues.)* When you're ready, you can ask them. In the meantime . . . just focus on my message. OK?

> *(Larry tries to speak, but his mouth just opens and closes.)*

GOD: *(Continues.)* Ooh, he's waking . . . Petra, we better do this now . . .

PETRA: OK! Well, Larry, I'm going to go over your reentry procedures. *(Takes his arm, starts to walk him offstage.)* Now it'll be just like waking up, only a little different. You might be a little sweaty, and you'll probably be very hungry. This is perfectly normal. It's OK to eat, but just light foods at first, veggies and dip, that sort of thing . . . *(Continues, quietly, as she leads him offstage.)*

GOD: Bye Larry! Thanks! And I meant it about not being a jerk, OK? Don't put up a billboard or anything, just communicate! Bye! Toodles!

> *(Petra returns. She and God look offstage after Larry.)*

PETRA: He was nice.

GOD: Good guy. So we have four more today?

PETRA: Six.

GOD: Ah. *(Beat.)* He's going to write a play, isn't he.

PETRA: They all do.

GOD: Damn. *(Beat.)* All right, bring on the next one.

END OF PLAY

Shades

Shades was first produced by Brass Tacks Theatre Company,
New York, N.Y., (Kevin Molesworth, Artistic Director) directed
by Brad Caswell, April, 2004.

CHARACTERS
> JOHN
>
> FREDA
>
> RICK

SETTING
> An apartment living room

· · ·

An apartment living room. There is a door leading outside, and a doorway to the bedroom. Three people are frozen in mid-laugh. Freda has her arm around John. Rick has a glass of milk in his hand. John and Rick are shaking hands. There is a softball among other knicknacks on a shelf nearby. There is a painted cube on the coffee table — it is painted a different color on every side: white, red, orange, yellow, green, and black. The white side is facing up. They unfreeze; all three are laughing uproariously. As it dies down, John looks straight out at the audience . . .

JOHN: White.
> *(The others pay no notice. He returns to the conversation.)*

FREDA: I'm afraid we don't really have much in the way of food to offer you . . .

JOHN: I think we have some cauliflower and dip in the fridge.

RICK: Freda always did have "bachelor refrigerator syndrome."

FREDA: *(Re: Rick's glass.)* I know . . . all we had was some milk . . .

JOHN: So, Rick . . . where's this new work of yours?

RICK: Right here . . . *(Indicates the cube.)*

JOHN: That's it? It looks like a . . . a block.

FREDA: Rick says it's a statement about all the different facets of experience. The colors of it . . .

RICK: Right. What we know and what we don't know. For instance, what color is the side that's face down? You have no way of knowing.

JOHN: Well . . . yeah . . .

RICK: And life is like that. You know, there are the three dimensions . . . up and down, forward and back, left and right. That's why I chose a cube.

JOHN: Um . . . well, that's . . .

FREDA: *(Puts her arm around John.)* John's more athletic than artistic.

RICK: Yes, I noticed the softball over there.

JOHN: Well, I don't know much about art. I think the last time I tried to draw was in third grade. And that was a polar bear in a snowstorm.

(They laugh, Rick politely.)

RICK: Plus there's the fourth dimension . . . Time. What happened in the past, what happens in the future? Only when we know every dimension of an experience can we truly understand it.

JOHN: *(Holding up video rental box.)* Well, I can tell you the immediate future. I rented *Snow White and the Seven Dwarves.* We're going to watch it tonight.

FREDA: It's our favorite movie.

RICK: I should get going.

JOHN: How much money can you make with this stuff, anyway?

FREDA: Oh millions — Rick's going to market them as Very Easy Rubik's Cubes!

(They laugh uproariously, as before; Rick moves to shake hands with John and they freeze in exactly the same position as before. The softball is replaced with red boxing gloves. The glass of milk is replaced with a glass of red wine. The cube is flipped so that the red side faces up. They unfreeze. The conversation plays out with the exact tone and movements as before, only the words change . . .)

FREDA: *(To the audience.)* Red.

(The others pay no notice. She returns to the conversation.)

FREDA: *(Continued.)* Half-hearted offer of food.

JOHN: Unknowingly symbolic mention of apples.

RICK: Reminiscence.

FREDA: Weak explanation for the wine.

JOHN: Change of subject!

RICK: Bid for approval . . . *(Indicates the cube.)*

JOHN: Complete confusion.

FREDA: Helpful explanation!

RICK: Meaningless art blather.

JOHN: Still confused.

RICK: More meaningless art blather?

JOHN: Still confused, but please no more art blather.

FREDA: *(Puts her arm around John.)* Defense of my man.

RICK: Nervous acknowledgement of the boxing gloves.

JOHN: Smug dismissal with banal childhood story about drawing a rooster.

(They laugh, Rick politely.)

RICK: Just a little more art blather.

JOHN: *(Holding up video rental box.)* Nipping it in the bud with *The Hunt for Red October.*

FREDA: Your cue to exit.

RICK: Taking cue.

JOHN: Last-minute cutting remark.

FREDA: Vicious dig!

(They laugh uproariously, as before; the men shake hands and all freeze. The boxing gloves are replaced with an basketball. The glass of red wine is replaced with a glass of orange juice. The cube is flipped so the orange side faces up. They unfreeze. The conversation plays out with the exact tone and movement as before, only the words change . . .)

RICK: *(To the audience.)* Orange.

FREDA: Do something polite. Offer him food. We have no food.

JOHN: I hope he doesn't want my carrot sticks. I was saving those.

RICK: I used to know her refrigerator. It was my refrigerator too.

FREDA: Jokingly mention the juice. Or not. Maybe I shouldn't have . . .

JOHN: Well, let's get on with the show and tell.

RICK: Here's something you won't understand . . . *(Indicates the cube.)*

JOHN: Surely that can't be it.

FREDA: John's going to say something stupid. Don't say something stupid John.

RICK: I can explain it, and you still won't understand it.

JOHN: He gets paid to do this?

RICK: This room looks exactly the same and completely different. My knick-knacks have simply been replaced with his.

JOHN: How long before this guy goes?

FREDA: *(Puts her arm around John.)* John's not awkward. Does anything make him awkward? Do I trust those who are never awkward?

RICK: *(Looking around, sees a basketball.)* Great, a basketball. He plays basketball. This guy and I are from two different planets.

JOHN: In third grade I tried to draw an orangutan. The other children laughed. I don't believe I've drawn anything since.

(They laugh, Rick politely.)

RICK: Freda is beautiful, the way women you can't have are beautiful. And yet . . .

JOHN: *(Holding up video rental box.)* I got *A Clockwork Orange* like Freda wanted. It seems an oddly violent choice for her. I wonder if it means anything.

FREDA: Ha! That'll make Rick wonder.

RICK: I need to talk to her. But not now.

JOHN: Would it be rude to put this in the VCR?

FREDA: Don't overplay it, Freda!

(Rick shoots her a look. They laugh uproariously, the men shake hands, they freeze. The boxing gloves are replaced with a banana. The glass of orange juice

is replaced with a glass of lemonade. The cube is flipped to yellow. They unfreeze.)

JOHN: *(To the audience.)* Yellow.

(The following happens very fast. They crouch like chimpanzees. They all are as realistically apelike as can be — it may be comical but it should also be brutal and violent.)

FREDA: *(Idly grooms John, pulling nits off of him and eating them.)* Oo oo!

JOHN: *(Offers Rick the banana.)* Eee?

RICK: *(Hoots.)*

FREDA: *(Referring to lemonade.)* Ooo ooo eep.

JOHN: *(Hoots.)* Rick

(Hoots, struts around the room, occasionally rising up to full height, waving arms: his mating dance.) Ee ee EEEE!

JOHN: *(Hoots, turns, keeps his body facing Rick.)*

FREDA: *(Hoots.)*

RICK: *(Raises his arms, screams like a monkey.)*

JOHN: *(Moves toward Rick, screams like a monkey, rises.)*

RICK: *(Hoots, charges, smacks John, then quickly backs off.)*

JOHN: *(Screams like a monkey.)*

FREDA: *(Puts her arm around John, screams like a monkey.)*

RICK: *(Runs to shelf, taps banana, runs back.)*

JOHN: *(Makes grotesque drawing motion.)* Oo ooo ee ee ee ee.

(They all laugh like monkeys.)

RICK: oo oo oo

JOHN: *(Holding up video rental box, it's Old Yeller.)* Oo oo ee ee.

FREDA: *(Screams like a monkey.)*

RICK: *(Ducks, cowers.)*

JOHN: *(Screams like a monkey.)*

FREDA: *(Hits him with the banana.)*

(They freeze. This time, Rick and John exit. The banana is replaced with a tennis ball. The cube is flipped so the green side faces up. This scene does NOT start as before. They unfreeze.)

FREDA: *(To the audience.)* Green.

(Then —)

FREDA: *(Continued.) (Greatly agitated, to offstage.)* For God's sake, get dressed! *(She is tucking in her clothes, too.)*

(Rick hops in from the bedroom, trying to run and pull his pants on at the same time, and failing miserably at both.)

RICK: I thought he worked till six —

FREDA: Usually! Oh, God, hurry!

RICK: Jacket!

FREDA: What?

RICK: My jacket!

(Freda runs back into the bedroom. Rick gets it from behind the couch.)

RICK: *(Continued.)* It's here! It's here!

(Freda reenters, Rick tries to put on his jacket, getting his arm in the wrong sleeve.)

FREDA: Forget it! Forget it! Just go!

(Rick moves to the front door. Freda pulls him back.)

FREDA: No, he's in the parking lot. He'll see you —

RICK: Pour me a drink.

FREDA: What?

RICK: A drink! Pour me a drink. I've come over to say hello.

FREDA: Brilliant.

(She hurriedly and shakily starts making a drink for Rick. It seems to take an agonizingly long time.)

RICK: What the hell are you doing?

FREDA: Making a mint julep!

RICK: What are you doing that for?!

FREDA: It was the first thing I could think of!

RICK: Just pour something in a glass for God sakes!

FREDA: I'm almost done!

RICK: And be mean to me.

FREDA: What?

RICK: Just be vaguely mean to me. Sarcastic. Otherwise he'll know what's up.

FREDA: That's good.

(She hands the drink to Rick and they affect relaxed poses just as John walks through the door. John carries a videotape of How Green Was My Valley.*)*

JOHN: Hey . . . oh hi!

FREDA: *(Going to kiss him)* Hi sweetie . . .

RICK: Hi . . .

FREDA: John, this is Rick . . . I told you about— . . . He came over to show me his latest work of art . . .

(John and Rick shake hands.)

JOHN: They let us out early —

FREDA: *(Simultaneously.)* I wanted him to meet you.

RICK: *(Simultaneously.)* Just wanted to stop by —

(They laugh uproariously — too much. They are now in the positions we've seen at the start and end of every scene.)

FREDA: I'm afraid we don't really have much in the way of food to offer you . . .

JOHN: I think we have some asparagus in the fridge . . .

(They freeze. The mint julep is replaced with a cup of coffee. The tennis ball is replaced with a "magic eight-ball" toy. The cube is flipped to black. They unfreeze.)

RICK: *(To the audience.)* Black.

FREDA: As it turned out, Rick and I didn't really have much in the way of anything to offer one another.

JOHN: Food kept spoiling in that fridge. I finally replaced it with a new one. Best to start fresh, anyway.

RICK: I saw Freda a few more times after that, but it only reminded us why it was over.

FREDA: I saw Rick one last time over coffee. We knew it was good-bye, but . . .

JOHN: I never suspected a thing. Maybe I wasn't very bright. Maybe I was happier.

RICK: *(Indicates the cube.)* I got a couple of big sculpture commissions, and that enabled me to move to Maine, which I'd always wanted to do.

JOHN: Two years later I married Freda. I was with her for the rest of my life.

FREDA: . . . You never really think it's going to be the last time you see a person.

RICK: I kept the cube with me in my studio.

JOHN: I made Senior Vice President at age forty-seven.

RICK: But no matter how much you look at things, or how many angles you see them from . . .

JOHN: We had three children. Three exquisitely beautiful children. All girls.

FREDA: *(Puts her arm around John.)* John's love was at a lower volume. No less heartfelt, just softer, quieter. It took me a while to hear it.

RICK: . . . you can never really know them. Not completely. One side is always face down, hidden.

JOHN: The middle one was the artist. She liked drawing ants. We put her pictures on the new refrigerator.

RICK: So I painted the last side of the cube black.

JOHN: *(Holding up video rental box.)* Their favorite movie was *Black Beauty.* They watched it hundreds of times. I liked watching them watch it.

FREDA: He doted on them.

RICK: To honor the mystery.

JOHN: When I died, I was surrounded by a loving family. One couldn't really ask for more.

FREDA: When I died, I realized that it was John who taught me how to love.

RICK: When I died, my knickknacks were simply replaced with another person's. The cube was taken from my house, and sold to someone else. But I don't think they ever really understood it . . .

(They freeze. The coffee is replaced with a glass of milk, the "magic eight-ball" with a softball, and the black cube with the colored one, white side up. They resume their places from the top of the play and freeze. Rick addresses the audience.)

RICK: *(Continued.)* White.

FREDA: I'm afraid we don't really have much in the way of food to offer you . . .

(The lights fade.)

END OF PLAY

Every Man

MICHAEL NIEDERMAN

Every Man was first produced in April of 2004 at Columbia University's Shapiro Studio. It featured Moana Niumeitolu as Savannah, Areshia McFarlin as Wendy, and Adam Tsekhman as Peter. It was directed by Mei-Yin Wang and Izumi Asakawa was the dramaturge.

CHARACTERS

> SAVANNAH
>
> WENDY
>
> PETER

SETTING

> A backyard

. . .

A backyard. Night. Savannah (fifteen) sits in her backyard. She looks up at the stars.

SAVANNAH: Look! That one's my star. The second star to the right. My mother gave it to me when I was just a little girl. It doesn't have a name. You can't name stars, silly. I'm sure they've got their own names. In star languages that we can't even understand. Like, one star might say to another star —

(She says something in "Star Language." It's probably high and piercing, but who knows?)

And then the other star would reply

(Again, a phrase in "Star Language.")

And us on Earth would have no idea what they're saying. Probably something about the price of neon gas or how they haven't seen any comets in seventy-one years.

(She talks in "Star Language" again, this time to the sky.)

SAVANNAH: I think I said hello. But you can never be too sure.

(Wendy [thirty-one] yells from inside the house.)

WENDY: *(Offstage.)* Savannah! Savannah! It's time to come inside!

SAVANNAH: In a minute, Mom.

WENDY: *(Offstage.)* It's time for bed!

SAVANNAH: In a minute!

(Wendy sticks her head out the window.)

WENDY: Did you did your homework?

SAVANNAH: Yes, Mom.

WENDY: I can check your books.

SAVANNAH: Check my books. I don't care.

WENDY: I will.

SAVANNAH: Go ahead.

(Wendy sticks her head back inside.)

WENDY: *(Offstage.)* Savannah!

SAVANNAH: What?

WENDY: *(Offstage.)* Where is your chemistry homework?

SAVANNAH: There wasn't any?

WENDY: *(Sticking her head back out.)* It's not too late to call your teacher.

SAVANNAH: Chemistry isn't until sixth period. I'll do it at lunch.

WENDY: *(Joining her daughter outside.)* I don't like you doing things at the last minute.

SAVANNAH: Mom! Can't you just — look at the stars with me. For a bit.

WENDY: OK. But no talking to the stars. It gives me a headache.

(The two of them sit in silence.)

SAVANNAH: Mom?

WENDY: Yeah, honey?

SAVANNAH: Do you think I'm pretty?

WENDY: Of course you are.

SAVANNAH: Then how come none of the boys like me?

WENDY: Well, you're still young. Give it time.

SAVANNAH: I've had nothing but time. I see the how the boys look at the other girls, the one's that have filled out more than I have. No one looks at me the same way.

WENDY: It's all in your head.

SAVANNAH: I'm not stupid, Mom. They don't look at me in the eyes. Or anywhere else.

WENDY: I think you're spending too much time looking at boys, and not enough at your books.

SAVANNAH: I try to be nice and different and cool. Do you think that it's because I try to talk to the stars?

(She says something again in "Star Language." Her mother hushes her.)

WENDY: Perhaps.

SAVANNAH: They don't look at me with want. I want to be wanted.

WENDY: Well, we all enjoy attention.

SAVANNAH: Mom, how old where you when you first got a boyfriend?

WENDY: Time for bed.

SAVANNAH: Mom.

WENDY: Well, I — I was older than you, that's for sure.

SAVANNAH: I'm fifteen.

WENDY: I know how old you are. Do we have to do this now?

SAVANNAH: Do what?

WENDY: The whole "facts of life" talk. You know, boys only want one thing.

SAVANNAH: Which one thing?

WENDY: You don't know?

SAVANNAH: Know what?

WENDY: Savannah, don't make me say it.

SAVANNAH: Yes, Mom. I know. We have HBO. I know all about sex.

WENDY: Well, that's just wonderful. And now you're depressed that you're not getting any. You're not getting any, are you?

SAVANNAH: I guess not.

WENDY: You guess? What are they teaching you kids in school?

SAVANNAH: I'm still a virgin!

WENDY: That's nice.

SAVANNAH: And I don't want to have sex. Yet.

WENDY: You've made your mother very proud.

SAVANNAH: But a boyfriend would be nice. I go to school every day and no one talks to me. I feel like no one knows me.

WENDY: I know you. And I know you've got to go to bed.

SAVANNAH: Mom — ?

WENDY: And no one's going to talk to you tomorrow because you're going to spend lunch alone in the library doing the Chemistry homework that you should have done tonight instead of making me worry that you're out getting pregnant. I'm going inside.

(Wendy goes inside.)

SAVANNAH: I could be cool. If I tried hard enough. I could get people to like me. If I tried hard enough. I could say the right things at all the right times and everybody would look up to me and then I would be cool. And all the boys would like me.

(Peter enters. He's a young man, incredibly handsome, and magical. Savannah falls under his spell.)

PETER: Hey. How you doing?

SAVANNAH: Hi. Do I know you?

PETER: No. I'm new. My name's Peter.

SAVANNAH: I've got to go inside.

PETER: It's not even eleven.

SAVANNAH: I've got school tomorrow.

PETER: You go to school too? Me too. I go to school all the time.

SAVANNAH: Of course I go to school. I'm only fifteen.

PETER: Only fifteen? There is no only fifteen. Fifteen is the cusp of the rest of your life. I'm Peter.

SAVANNAH: I'm Savannah.

PETER: Savannah. Such a nice name.

SAVANNAH: Oh, I don't like it. Makes me sound like an old lady.

PETER: You don't look like an old lady to me. You look . . . You look fifteen.
I like fifteen. It's a cusp. I like cusps.

SAVANNAH: Cusps?

PETER: It means the edge. Just after something, but right before something else.
That's where you are, Savannah. You're on the cusp.

SAVANNAH: My birthday's not for another eight months.

PETER: I wasn't talking about chronological age. Though I so do love fifteen.

SAVANNAH: How old did you say you were again?

PETER: I didn't.

SAVANNAH: Well, how old are you?

PETER: Eighteen?

SAVANNAH: So you're a senior?

PETER: Yeah, I'm a senior.

SAVANNAH: Do you know where you're going to college yet? Because I'm just
starting that whole process. My mom says I need to get my grades up and
do some more extracurricular activities if I want to go anywhere good,
but I don't know if I want to go to college yet. I might work summers
and save for a trip to Europe for a year and then worry about the rest of
my life. I mean, what is college, anyway, but a place where you study the
work of a bunch of dead straight white guys who —

PETER: Shhhh. You talk too much.

(Silence. She fiddles with the hem of her skirt.)

PETER: That's why you can't get a boyfriend.

SAVANNAH: I do that sometimes when I get nervous.

PETER: You need to listen more.

(Silence.)

SAVANNAH: Hey, you want to hear me talk to a star?

PETER: No. I want to see you without your shirt on.

SAVANNAH: What?

PETER: You've been wanting to ever since I sat down. Right?

SAVANNAH: No!

PETER: Then why can't you stop fiddling with the hem of your skirt and the
neck of you blouse?

SAVANNAH: Because it's hot. And you're making me nervous. The way you're
staring at me.

PETER: I thought that's what you wanted. Boys to stare at you. Instead of passing you by as they look for the girls who put out. Really know you. Savannah, I think I know you.

SAVANNAH: You just met me.

PETER: I know that no one understands you, and it tears you up inside. That you've got hopes and dreams bigger than this town, of seaside resorts and continental breakfasts with tall men whose hair falls into their eyes.

SAVANNAH: What's a continental breakfast?

PETER: It's just like a regular one, except with a fruit plate. Forget about breakfast. What do you want to do?

SAVANNAH: I don't know. My mom thinks I should go to college and become a doctor or lawyer or —

PETER: I'm not talking about what your mother wants.

SAVANNAH: I don't know what I want.

PETER: I'd like to kiss you. If that's OK.

SAVANNAH: I guess so. A quick one. I've got to go inside soon.

PETER: Well, we can't keep Mother waiting.

(They kiss. Savannah starts to swoon into his arms, but stops herself at the last moment.)

PETER: How did that feel?

SAVANNAH: OK, I guess.

PETER: Did it make you feel warm inside, in your stomach? So delightfully warm, yet itchy, and all you can think to do is reach down and scratch?

SAVANNAH: Do you want me to take off my shirt?

PETER: Savannah, I thought you'd never ask.

(She starts to unbutton her shirt.)

(Wendy enters.)

WENDY: Savannah. It's time to go inside.

PETER: Just one minute, Mom.

WENDY: Now.

(Savannah does.)

WENDY: I think you should go now, too.

PETER: Where should I go to?

WENDY: Wherever people like you come from.

PETER: I've always been here. Don't you remember me?

WENDY: Should I?

PETER: I'd feel real blue if you didn't remember me.

WENDY: I've known men like you. Men who think they can prey on naïve girls like my daughter.

PETER: She's not that naïve. She's young, sure, but there's a real fire inside that one, just waiting to burn.

(Wendy slaps him.)

WENDY: I told you never to talk like that again.

PETER: You do remember me. I thought your memory was fading with old age, Wendy.

WENDY: I'm not that old. How come you look the same?

PETER: I'll always look like this. This is what I am.

WENDY: You should go now. And never come back.

PETER: Don't you want to talk?

WENDY: I've got nothing to say to you.

PETER: I thought we spent good times together.

WENDY: You don't have to live with the regret. You never had to.

PETER: You don't know what I live with.

(She starts to go inside.)

PETER: Wendy, I've missed you.

WENDY: She's just a child.

PETER: So were you.

WENDY: That was a long time ago.

PETER: I remember we used to meet in the woods behind your house. We'd lie under a tree all afternoon and you'd tell me stories of what your life would be like.

WENDY: No one ever listened to me back then.

PETER: How many listen to you now?

WENDY: I don't think you should come around here anymore.

PETER: One last dance.

WENDY: No. Not that.

PETER: Please. Just one. And then I'll go.

(He snaps his fingers. A slow, sad torch song plays. Maybe "Lady Stardust" by David Bowie.)

(He holds his hands out for Wendy. She hesitates for a moment, then collapses in his arms. They dance.)

WENDY: God, I forgot how good this felt.

PETER: I never meant to hurt you. You or anyone close to you.

WENDY: I just missed you so much.

PETER: But you moved on. It happens. I'm used to it now.

WENDY: Your arms. I feel so safe in your arms.

PETER: I could stay here. I could keep you safe.

WENDY: Ever since I knew you I've been running from you. Running from how safe I feel in your arms.

PETER: The three of us could be a family. You and me and Savannah. I could make you all happy.

WENDY: Happy.

PETER: Happy. Me and all my girls. And if Savannah were to have a daughter, we'll be happier still.

(She stays in his arms for a moment. She then pushes him away. The music stops.)

WENDY: No! No, you are not going to do this to me again.

PETER: Wendy, come on. Remember how you loved me? Don't you want Savannah to have that love?

WENDY: You keep away from me. And you keep away from my daughter.

PETER: But there are so many things I could teach her.

WENDY: Life will happen to her no matter what. You will not make her rush. My daughter won't live with the same regret I've had.

PETER: I'll always be a part of you.

WENDY: That part of me's been dead for a long time.

PETER: Do you really want me to go?

(Wendy says nothing. Peter goes to leave.)

WENDY: Peter?

PETER: Yes, Wendy?

WENDY: Say hello to the stars for me.

PETER: You're all we ever talk about.

(Peter leaves. Wendy looks up at the sky. The music swells again. Wendy says something in "Star Language.")

(Blackout.)

END OF PLAY

Molly Whuppie

DON NIGRO

CHARACTERS
>   RING: a large blind man
>   MOLLY: an orphan girl
>   CARLY: Ring's daughter

SETTING
>   A remote farmhouse in Pendragon County, Ohio, some years ago. All we
>   see is an old bed in Molly's room, with a small nightstand beside it.

• • •

*Sound of a ticking clock. Night in the old farmhouse. Sound of an owl hoot-
ing. Then somewhere the moon emerges from behind a cloud revealing Molly,
a young girl in a white nightgown, lying in her bed, visible in a shaft of moonlight coming in a window we can't see, with darkness all around. Sound of
a door creaking open in the darkness, and heavy footsteps. Then Ring moves
into the edge of the moonlight, a large blind man.*

RING: Are you sleeping, Molly Whuppie?

MOLLY: Don't call me that. I hate it when you call me that. Why do you call
me that?

RING: For the poor orphan girl out of the fairy tale, killed the giant and stole
his gold. Did your mother never read you that story?

MOLLY: No. She never did.

RING: Well, that's a shame. Why aren't you sleeping, Molly Whuppie? Molly
Whuppie needs her beauty sleep. How can she be the sleeping beauty in
the fairy tale if she stays up all night listening to the owls?

MOLLY: How can I sleep with a blind man jabbering in my room?

RING: It's ungrateful to comment upon a man's infirmity, who took you in when
your mother died. Who else would have done that, Molly? Nobody in
the world but me, that's who.

MOLLY: You got money enough for it.

RING: And what money would that be?

MOLLY: You know what money. You keep it in a wooden box in your room.
You got money in the will for taking me in.

RING: *(Moving closer to her as he speaks, feeling his way to the bed.)* Not enough.
And you eat up my money, day by day. Every day you live you eat up
more of the money I got to keep you. What will I do when the money's
gone? How will I feed my own daughter Carly? She's all I have, since her
mother died. This is how it is, Molly Whuppie. Two dead sisters, her

mother and yours. And me left with an extra mouth to feed, and you eating up the money every day. It's lonely here, without my wife.

MOLLY: You were cruel to your wife. You beat your wife. I've heard it said you strangled her in her bed.

RING: Who said that?

MOLLY: The owls whispered it to me.

RING: Well, you know, Molly, you shouldn't listen to the owls, for they're only good at asking questions and devouring mice, and also, Molly dear, a man who would strangle his own wife in her bed would most likely not hesitate to strangle a poor slut of an orphan girl who made fun of his affliction and was eating up all his money like rats eat oats. A man like that might just creep into a poor girl's room one night and put his hands around her throat and squeeze until she stopped flopping about, and then put her in a sack like a cat and bury her by the windmill. That's what a man might do, if he was that sort of a fellow. For blind men have strong hands, Molly. You might want to keep that in mind when you open your pretty mouth to speak on an autumn night, the next time you're talking to the owls.

MOLLY: Don't stand so close. I can smell the liquor on your breath.

RING: I smell of liquor, and tobacco, yes, and God knows what else, dead animals, I suppose, but you always smell so sweet, Molly. What is it that makes you always smell so sweet?

MOLLY: It's just vanilla extract. My mother gave it to me. It was my mother's.

RING: You smell like my wife. I miss my wife. I could see once, you know. But I can't remember her face. I've an overpowering urge to touch your hair. *(Ring reaches out his big hands toward Molly. But just as he's about to touch her, his daughter Carly steps into the edge of the moonlight, also wearing a white nightgown.)*

CARLY: Papa?

RING: *(Pulling his hands back.)* Yes, child? What is it?

CARLY: What are you doing in here?

RING: Just tucking your cousin Molly up tight in her bed, dearie. She's had a nightmare a giant come into her room in the night and tried to strangle her, didn't you, Molly?

MOLLY: Yes.

RING: She's a clever girl, Molly Whuppie is, but she has bad dreams, and a streak of darkness in her, don't you? Got it from her dead mother, perhaps. There was a deep one, she was.

MOLLY: Don't you talk about my mother.

RING: Yes, some things are better not spoken of, I suppose. But once I recall

your mother said to me, not long before she died, she said, look out for my little Molly, she said. She's beautiful, but she's got a spot of darkness in her soul. God help me, she said. I've never been able to love her.
(Pause.)
Well, I'm going out to dig me a hole by the windmill.

CARLY: To dig a hole? Papa, why would you want to dig a hole at this time of night?

RING: To bury a dead stray bitch I had to strangle, dear. It was a sad thing, but it had to be done, for there was nothing in the house for her to eat.

CARLY: But can't you do that in the morning, Papa?

RING: When a man has lost his wife, and can't sleep, he might as well go out and dig a hole. You get back to your own bed and go to sleep, sweetheart. Your cousin Molly needs a good, long sleep. That's what she needs. Now, give me a kiss good night.
(Carly kisses him on the cheek.)
That's my girl. And you, Molly. Give your Uncle Ring a kiss good night.
(Molly hesitates. Then she kisses him lightly on the cheek.)
There's a good girl. Is it true you're a pretty girl, Molly? Or was that your mother's lie?

CARLY: Molly's beautiful, Papa. She's like a girl out of a fairy tale. She's the most beautiful girl there ever was.

RING: I thought as much. Except for you, of course, my love. Except for you.
(He touches Carly's head, then starts away.)
Now, you go back to your own room and get to sleep, Carly, my love.

CARLY: Yes, Papa. I will.

RING: You're a sweet girl, Carly. Simple and sweet, and you're all my world, you know. You're all my world and everything in it. Everything in it.
(Ring goes out, disappearing into the darkness.)

CARLY: You mustn't let Papa upset you. He's not the same since Mama died. He drinks more than before. I worry so about him. But he's been better since you came, Molly. I'm so happy you've come to live with us. It's not nearly as lonely with you here. And I've always wanted a sister. Did you always want a sister, Molly?

MOLLY: I always wanted a father. I never had one.

CARLY: Yes. I'm a lucky girl to have a father. It's cold tonight. Can I get into bed and cuddle with you for a while?

MOLLY: I don't know, Carly. Your father might not like it. He's in an odd mood tonight.

CARLY: *(Getting under the covers with Molly.)* The full moon makes men strange, Mother said. It makes them turn to wolves. Just for a minute, let me curl up with you. I'm so sleepy I can hardly hold my chin up, and it's so nice to snuggle up with you. You're so warm, and you smell so good. You smell like my mother.

MOLLY: It's just vanilla extract. You can have some, if you like. Here. *(Molly gets a little brown bottle from the nightstand, takes the cork out, puts her finger to the bottle, then touches Carly under her ears and at her throat.)* Just here, and here, and here at your throat.

CARLY: *(Taking Molly's hand and kissing it.)* You have such pretty hands, and you're so kind to me. I love you, Molly.

MOLLY: Well, that's an odd feeling, to be loved. I hardly know what to make of it. I think it is always dangerous to love.

CARLY: But it's more dangerous not to. I've been so lonely here. I just want to curl up with you like kittens and fall asleep forever. It's so strange with Papa now. He drinks so much, and talks to himself, and sits up late by the fire, mumbling at nobody. Papa loves me. I'm all he has. He never cried when Mama died, but he cried when I was sick. It scares me sometimes that he loves me so. It's a terrible thing to be loved so much. Do you know what I mean, Molly?

MOLLY: No. I don't know what you mean.

CARLY: It's a burden, to be loved too much. Did you ever want to run away? I'd like to run away to Spain. They have the best windmills in Spain. Sometimes I dream about them.

MOLLY: You're thinking of the Low Countries. They have windmills in the Low Countries. And they turn in the night and make creaking sounds like the bedsprings, and moaning sounds like the owls.

CARLY: What a strange girl you are, Molly. I love you because you're so strange, and private. Sometimes I wonder, what is she always thinking of? You're like my father that way.

MOLLY: I'm not like your father.

CARLY: You are. There's something in your eyes that's just like him. I don't know what it is, but I know it's there.

MOLLY: Maybe some day I'll take the money from the wooden box in your father's room and run away to Spain.

CARLY: When you do, will you take me with you?

MOLLY: A person can only go to Spain alone, I think. Now, you should get back in your own bed, before your father comes home and finds you here. He'll be angry with you then.

CARLY: I know, but it feels so nice here. Just a few minutes more. I feel so safe with you. I've never felt so safe with anybody in my life, since Mama died.

MOLLY: *(Stroking Carly's hair.)* Carly, do you think that your father — do you think that your father is a person who — do you think he's someone who's capable of hurting somebody?

CARLY: *(Drifting off to sleep.)* Who would he hurt?

MOLLY: I don't know. Anybody. Do you think he really would?

CARLY: He's very strong. He always teased Mama that some day he would kill her. My father likes to tease the girls. He has very strong hands. He's very good at strangling rabbits.

MOLLY: Carly? Wake up, dear, and go back to your bed. Carly?

(Carly is asleep.)

Poor foolish child. How stupid you are to love me. How stupid you are. *(She kisses Carly tenderly on the forehead. Sound of the owl. Then, heavy footsteps approaching in the darkness, and the creaking of a door. A moment. Then Ring shuffles into the light.)*

RING: Are you sleeping, Molly Whuppie? Can I hear you sleeping now? I've started digging a wonderful hole by the windmill.

(He moves toward the bed slowly. Molly watches, motionless.)

Sweet breath of the sleeping beauty. Sweet, scent of the sleeping girl. Many's the night I've lain awake, listening to my poor dead wife sleeping beside me. A blind man's at home in the darkness. You smell so much like my wife. I have an overpowering urge to touch your hair.

(He reaches one hand down. It comes to rest on Carly's hair.)

I wouldn't hurt you for the world, Molly. I never hurt the rabbits. I do it very quickly. They never know what happened. The secret is to caress them first.

(As Ring's knee comes to rest on the mattress, Molly slips quietly out of bed.)

Just one snap and then it's over. And then you know the darkness that I know.

(Molly hesitates, then creeps away into the dark. Ring puts his hands around Carly's neck and squeezes. The moon goes behind a cloud. Darkness.)

END OF PLAY

It's Called Development

ANNE PHELAN

A workshop of the play was directed by Cindy Ohanian for
"Sin and Virtue," for the Playwright/Director Laboratory (Julie
Fei-Fan Balzer, Director) at the Looking Glass Theatre, New
York City, in December 2001. A later version was directed by
James P. Robinson as part of "The Sacred and the Profane" at
the NewGate Theatre, Providence, R.I. in 2004.

CHARACTERS

> AMY: executive director of a large charitable foundation; thirties
>
> MS. TEUFEL: a mysterious potential donor with close connections to Satan; looks twenties, but as old as time
>
> KASPARINA: Ms. Teufel's willing and able assistant; looks twenties to thirties, but at least as old as the cockroach

SETTING

> Ms. Teufel's lair, somewhere in Lower Manhattan. The present.

•   •   •

> *Ms. Teufel's lair — a realistic corporate office, expensively furnished. Kasparina enters, leading Amy.*

AMY: *(Looking around.)* Isn't it a little dark in here?

KASPARINA: Low light is always flattering.

AMY: *(Coughs.)* You could offer me a beverage.

KASPARINA: The delivery didn't come.

AMY: Spring water, juice, a latte —

KASPARINA: Nope.

AMY: *(Reluctantly.)* Poland Spring?

KASPARINA: They're working on the boiler. There's not even tap water.

AMY: *(Pulls at her collar.)* It's warm in here.

KASPARINA: I don't think so.

AMY: Maybe I'm coming down with something.
> *(Recoiling.)*
> Something smells like sulfur.

KASPARINA: Aren't you the sensitive plant? I wouldn't want your job. Professionalized begging, that's all fund-raising is.

AMY: It's called "development."

KASPARINA: Yeah, and George Washington called the outhouse the "necessary." Don't make it smell any sweeter.

AMY: *(Belittling.)* One can't expect someone of your kind to understand.

KASPARINA: It just makes you feel important. Throwing galas, getting your picture in the *Times Sunday Style* section —

AMY: That's hard work. Certainly hell on my skin.

KASPARINA: You're a debutante! And you're paid a fortune.

AMY: I was on the cover of *Town and Country* last month. I don't need to justify myself to some nouveau riche's secretary. I checked — your boss isn't even in the Social Register.

KASPARINA: She don't need to be, honey.

AMY: Do you speak to every guest like that?

KASPARINA: What's the difference between you and the guy outside Citibank with the paper cup? At least he's the genuine article. You people gussy it up with cocktails and expensive stationery.

AMY: You're too common to understand. Is Ms. T — Too — how do you pronounce it?

KASPARINA: Toy-ful.

AMY: Sounds foreign. Is she here? I'm very busy.

KASPARINA: Sure. Can't you smell her?

(Amy sniffs, and coughs. Kasparina laughs.)

AMY: *(Nearly choking.)* What — is — that — stench?

KASPARINA: I've gotten used to it. Along with everything else.

AMY: What do you mean?

KASPARINA: You're awfully frail to be such a big honcho. How'd you get where you are?

AMY: I inherited G.I.G. from my uncle.

KASPARINA: Huh?

AMY: G. I. G.: Giving Is Good. It used to be the Orphans Benevolent Society, but that sounded so over. We hired an image consultant to come up with something sexier.

MS. TEUFEL: *(Enters wearing a business suit. To Amy.)* I apologize profusely! It simply couldn't be helped. Kasparina's been entertaining you?

AMY: *(Looking at Kasparina.)* That's your name?

MS. TEUFEL: *(To Kasparina.)* Hold all my calls. We mustn't be disturbed. Amy's time is precious.

KASPARINA: *(With a grin.)* Sure.

MS. TEUFEL: And don't listen over the intercom.

(Disappointed, Kasparina exits.)

Amy, do sit down. I've been so looking forward to meeting you. What a darling suit you're wearing!

AMY: *(Opening her expensive briefcase.)* I've brought some materials —

MS. TEUFEL: *(Waves it away.)* Nonsense! Completely unnecessary. You're among friends here.

AMY: *(Surprised.)* But our programs —

MS. TEUFEL: All I need is a little tête-à-tête with you.

(Amy closes up her briefcase.)

How would 2.5 million be?

AMY: *(Ecstatic.)* Fabulous!

MS. TEUFEL: There's one teeny little condition.

AMY: Anything you want! Do you know how many orphans we can send to school with that money?

MS. TEUFEL: My condition — it's so small it's barely worth mentioning.

AMY: What?

MS. TEUFEL: All you have to do is resign your position.

AMY: What?!

MS. TEUFEL: Tell your Board you need a change. They'll understand.

AMY: I've met eccentric donors in my time, but —

MS. TEUFEL: It is my money. I have a right to say how it's spent.

AMY: That's not fair.

MS. TEUFEL: I'm afraid it's the only way. It would be for the good of the orphans —

AMY: *(Losing it.)* It's mine! My foundation, my orphans, my —

MS. TEUFEL: *(Stands.)* Sorry.

AMY: I'll resign my job but stay on the Board.

MS. TEUFEL: I'll have to insist on no more contact.

AMY: But what'll I do?

MS. TEUFEL: I don't know.

AMY: What's in this for you?

MS. TEUFEL: It's a little embarrassing, but I've got too much money.

AMY: There's no such thing as too much money. Do you mind if I ask where yours comes from?

MS. TEUFEL: Drugs, arms sales, child prostitution in the Far East.
(Amy is floored.)
The banks are watching me too carefully. I need to get rid of some, in a productive way that won't arouse any suspicion from the S.E.C. G.I.G. is perfect.

AMY: My family have been philanthropists for a hundred years. How could I stoop to your level?

MS. TEUFEL: We're all in business of one kind or another. Does it really matter where the money comes from?

AMY: Of course.

MS. TEUFEL: The Roosevelts got started in the Chinese opium trade. John D. Rockefeller's father wandered around upstate selling bottles of snake oil. I'm not sure I see the difference.

AMY: I do.

MS. TEUFEL: College tuition could be $75,000 a year by the time your little orphans turn eighteen. What if there's no City College by then? Can you bear the responsibility for keeping them down?

AMY: *(Whistling in the dark.)* I'll find the money somewhere else.

MS. TEUFEL: *(Gently.)* It's not the '90s anymore. You need to take this money.

AMY: I'll look bad.

MS. TEUFEL: No, you'll go out with a bang.

AMY: I'll disappear.

MS. TEUFEL: You can do a press release saying you got me to give the foundation the money.

AMY: Really?

MS. TEUFEL: The *Times* may pick it up. Certainly *The Chronicle of Philanthropy.*

AMY: *(Caving.)* Well, it would be for the orphans —

MS. TEUFEL: *(Lovingly.)* Oh, Amy, you've so completely surpassed my expectations. *(Calling.)* Kasparina! She failed with flying colors! Take her away. *(To Amy.)* You really have made my day. I get your soul, and all those little orphans stay ignorant.

AMY: I need to get back to the office.

(Kasparina enters.)

MS. TEUFEL: *(To Kasparina.)* Take her home.

AMY: But I have work to do —

MS. TEUFEL: Not your home, our home.

AMY: *(Kasparina takes Amy's arm.)* What are you doing?

MS. TEUFEL: We're putting you with your own kind, that's all. Don't fret, you'll know oodles of people in Hell. *(To Kasparina.)* Tell the Duchess of Windsor and Andy Warhol they've got to stop tormenting the goose that lays the golden eggs. And when you've finished settling Amy in, bring in the next victim.

(Kasparina and Amy exit.)

END OF PLAY

An Ongoing Examination of the True Meaning of Life

S. W. SENEK

This play was performed at the 2005 New York Fifteen Minute Play Festival at the American Globe Theatre. It was directed by S.W. Senek. The cast was as follows: Playwright: Sandra Holguin; He: Joel Stigliano; She: Krysta L. Randles. This play was also presented at the Last Frontier Theatre Conference in Valdez, Alaska (2005). It was then produced there in 2006. It was directed by Codie Costello. The cast was as follows: Playwright: Krista M. Schwarting; He: Jeff McCamish; She: Eleanor Janecek Delaney

CHARACTERS
    PLAYWRIGHT
    HE
    SHE

SETTING
    Playwright's office

NOTES
    As the play progresses, He and She slowly become frustrated as they struggle to be together — without the help of the Playwright.

TEMPO OF THE PLAY
    Allegro

• • •

Lights up on the Playwright who sits in front of a computer. Playwright contemplates for a moment, takes a sip of coffee, contemplates again then begins.

PLAYWRIGHT: Working title for this Play about true love, *(Beat.) Love at . . . the Coffee Shop.* Lights up in a coffee shop. We see a table.
(Man puts the table onstage. Lights up on a table.)
Strike that, a park bench.
(Lights out on the table.)
New working title, *Love at . . . the Park.*
(Man removes table.)
Lights up on a bench.
(Man places a bench onstage. Lights up on the bench.)
It is a dreary fall day; a small amount of leaves surrounding the bench.
(Woman enters and drops a few leaves.)
Scratch that — it's a bright and crisp fall day —
(It becomes brighter. Woman runs offstage and returns with more leaves. Man is following her holding one leaf.)
and a large amount of leaves surrounding the bench.
(Woman drops more leaves. Man drops his single leaf and exits.)
Perhaps that's too many.
(Woman picks his leaf up and begins to exit.)
That's nice — except there should be some leaves on the bench to make it look authentic.

(Woman returns, picks some leaves up and drops them on the bench.)

Nope, I was wrong. That looks messy.

(Woman returns to the bench frustrated and knocks the leaves off then exits.)

Better.

Enter Man — "He."

(Man enters.)

No.

(Man turns and exits.)

Yes, He enters.

(He enters again.)

Man carries a newspaper, sports a well-made fedora with an overcoat, whistling.

(Man does this.)

No hat, keep the overcoat and the paper — forget the whistling. He hums.

(Man does this.)

No, drop the paper — let's try a book

(Woman tosses him a book.)

and add glasses.

(Man pulls out glasses and puts them on.)

The man rests on the bench and begins to read.

(He sits.)

No.

(Man stands.)

The man looks at his watch then sits and reads. No, looks around before reading. Smiles. Frowns — the man is blind.

(Man drops the book and blindly feels outward.)

No, he can see.

He's blind

(He goes to the ground and feels for the book.)

— which makes it difficult to read. Alright, he can see, but he's losing his sight.

(Man struggles to read.)

Enter woman — "She" — skipping hurriedly.

(Woman enters skipping.)

Back up.

(She skips backwards.)

How about a slow skip without purpose — or with purpose, but without skipping.

(She does this.)

She wears a dress, carries a basket, and pulls out a light blue sweater.
(She does this.)
No, red.
(Begins to pull a red sweater from her basket.)
No, green.
(She pulls a green sweater from her basket.)
— let's go blue.
(She pulls out the blue sweater . . . again.)
Perfect. She enters and searches for a place to sit.
(She stands behind him searching to one side, then the other.)
No, she doesn't search, she knows where to sit — the same bench she sits at every day at lunch.
(She sits.)
She has knitting tools. No, He has knitting tools, She has the book.
(They trade.)
She opens the book to page one — the middle of the book — she's almost finished with the book. He turns toward her. Away. Toward. Away. Toward. Yes. She looks back — she ignores him. She loves him.
(They embrace.)
She hates him.
(She stands and slaps him.)
She doesn't know him. He speaks.

HE: *(Southern voice. He stands up and continues knitting.)* Howdy ma'am!
PLAYWRIGHT: Spits to the side and smears the tobacco drizzle romantically.
  (He does this — well, as romantic as one can smear tobacco drizzle.)
HE: How about a wet one, right here.
  (Points to his mouth where the drizzle was.)
PLAYWRIGHT AND SHE: Yuck.
PLAYWRIGHT: Try that again.
HE: *(Guido voice. Sits and still knits.)* Aye, baby — how you doin'? You wanna touch my hairy back?
PLAYWRIGHT: Less is more.
HE: *(Plain.)* Hello.
PLAYWRIGHT: She nods back. No, waves. No, she flips him off. She speaks.
SHE: LEAVE ME ALONE!
  (He protects himself by holding the knitting needles together as a cross.)
PLAYWRIGHT: She's nicer — and English.
SHE: How about an old romp on the rump?
HE: Eh?

SHE: Sex.

HE: Yes!

PLAYWRIGHT: No — too soon. Drop the accent.

SHE: *(Plain, somewhat shy.)* Hello.

PLAYWRIGHT: They acknowledge each other. He ponders how to start a conversation.

(He's speechless.)

Awkward moment. Uncomfortable silence.

(Just the sound of knitting needles tapping against one another.)

He looks at her legs. She smiles. He examines her breast. She doesn't smile. He looks up her dress.

HE: Peek-a-boo — Peek-a-boo!

PLAYWRIGHT: She hits him over the head. Scratch that — he holds up his knitting job —

SHE: What is it?

HE: It's lingerie! For my grandmother!

PLAYWRIGHT: It's a scarf.

HE: A scarf. I love knitting! My father and I knit together every Monday night.

PLAYWRIGHT: No.

HE: I'm knitting you underpants.

PLAYWRIGHT: No. Forget the knitting. Read the newspaper. He speaks again.

HE: How much can one endure, I ask? Cover to cover, it's endless. The whole world's at war, the economy's down, there's murder in the city! Doom! Doom! DOOM!

PLAYWRIGHT: Too pessimistic.

HE: *I like to read the personal ads upside down.*

(He turns paper upside down.)

PLAYWRIGHT: That doesn't make sense.

HE: I find it utterly repulsive when black newsprint gets on my fingers? *(Wipes his fingers on her.)*

SHE: It turns me on.

(She brushes her hand against his face, causing his glasses to slide crooked.)

PLAYWRIGHT: No, she agrees with him.

SHE: *(Very quick ramble.)* Yes, especially if I'm wearing white. Like yesterday, I'm wearing my white dress shoes with the pink flower on the toes, my matching white pants — which took me all day to find at the clothing store — not to mention my white blouse, which I paid way too much for. I would've had the white jacket except they were sold out — Do you believe that? A sale on white jackets and they're sold out. I asked for a rain check on the item. They said they couldn't order any more. I ask why, they said "It didn't sell, which is why we had the sale."

PLAYWRIGHT AND HE: Right.

PLAYWRIGHT: Forget the newspaper, he's knitting again. He sees her book.

HE: *Catch 22?*

SHE: Yes.

HE: That was the worst book I ever read.

SHE: This is my favorite book. It's my fourth time reading it.

PLAYWRIGHT: No.

HE: I love that book, it reminds me of my college days — that's when I read it.

SHE: It reminds me of shooting my first husband. He was reading it when I shot him.
    (She slams the book shut.)

PLAYWRIGHT: Ouch.

HE: Great book.

SHE: Is it?

HE: *(Can't contain himself.)* Yosarian doesn't have to fly the mission — he lives! He lives! Isn't that wonderful? Rejoice! He lives!

SHE: Thanks for ruining the ending.
    (Slams book shut.)

PLAYWRIGHT: Back that up. He has a book as well.

HE: Great book.

SHE: I know. I can't stop reading it. What are you reading?

HE: *How to Pick up Women in the Park.*

PLAYWRIGHT: Too direct.

HE: *How to Have Confidence. (Beat.)* I think I wet myself.

PLAYWRIGHT: How embarrassing.

HE: A book of poems.

SHE: I despise poetry.

PLAYWRIGHT: She loves poetry.

SHE: I love poetry.

PLAYWRIGHT: He reads her some.

HE: *(Optional: An underscore of Beatnik poetry music.)*
    You, you, you.
    Smell.
    Yucky, stinky, stinky — like
    Big, brown, brown, big cow.
    You, you, you.
    (End music.)

PLAYWRIGHT: Perhaps a little more romantic.

HE: *(Very romantic voice.)*

    You, you, you,
    Fresh roses.
    My heart, beats a racehorse —
    My racehorse.
    It calls out for
    You, you, you.

SHE: That inspires me to do an interpretive dance.

    (Splashy galloping music. She gallops like a horse.)

PLAYWRIGHT AND HE: NO!

SHE: I have a slight hearing loss, but I'm sure it was nice poetry.

HE: Hi, I'm Don Fluedenflanker.

SHE: Ron Fladenfocker.

HE: Don Fluedenflanker.

SHE: Tom Fuckenflicker.

HE: Don Fluedenflanker!

SHE: Won Winkywanker.

PLAYWRIGHT: Suddenly she hears.

SHE: It's a miracle! I can hear!

PLAYWRIGHT: He changes name.

HE: Hi my name is Upenschtiemer van Blottenpoppenschtiemer.

PLAYWRIGHT: No.

HE: Hi my name is John. You?

SHE: My hooker name is Iwanna Bendover.

    (She turns around showing her rear, he brings his hand back to slap it —.)

HE: Yes.

PLAYWRIGHT: No.

SHE: I'm Mary. Nice to meet you John.

    (They shake hands.)

HE: Boy this day sucks — besides my athlete's foot acting up, I have contagious genital warts that itch like crazy.

SHE: You too?

    (They stop shaking hands.)

PLAYWRIGHT: No.

HE: The color of your hair —

SHE: Yes?

HE: It reminds me of my dog.

    (She stands and slaps him.)

PLAYWRIGHT: No.

HE: It's the perfect color.

SHE: Thanks. I saturate it in raw eggs every night.

PLAYWRIGHT: Delete that.

SHE: It's a wig — I'm really a man. Do you want to see my penis?

PLAYWRIGHT AND HE: NO!

SHE: Thank you. It's natural — from my mother's side.

HE: Great. I hope I'm not too forward, but I noticed you here during summer.

SHE: You have?

HE: Yes. I wanted to talk to you. But . . .

SHE: Yes?

HE: Well, I'm nervous.

SHE: What's to be nervous about?

HE: That you wouldn't like me for who I am.

SHE: And who are you?

HE: A convicted killer —

PLAYWRIGHT: No.

SHE: What's there to be nervous about?

HE: I wear adult diapers.

PLAYWRIGHT: No.

SHE: What's there to be nervous about?

HE: I have an uncontrollable lisp.

SHE: You do?

HE: Yeth. *(Translation: Yes.)*

SHE: Tho do I! *(Translation: So do I!)*

HE: That'th terrific! *(Translation: That's terrific!)*

SHE: Thplendid. *(Translation: Splendid.)*

HE: Thuper. *(Translation: Super.)*

SHE: Motht guyth think it'th a turnoff. *(Translation: Most guys think it's a turnoff.)*

HE: Thame here. Exthept the "guy" part. *(Translation: Same here except the "guy" part.)*

PLAYWRIGHT: No — he drops the lisp — she keeps it.

HE: The truth is I'm narcoleptic.

SHE: Thplendid! *(Translation: Splendid!)* Me too!
    (He slowly falls asleep.)

SHE: What'sth the chanthes of thith happening! Finding thomeone who understhandths! Maybe thaths why I never realithed you were thitting right bethide me becauthe I fell athleep too. Maybe thith ith why I can't finith reading my book. *(Translation: What are the chances of this happening — finding someone who understands? Maybe that's why I've never realized you were sitting beside me here at this park bench because I fell asleep too. Maybe this is why I can't finish reading my book.)*

(She falls asleep.)

PLAYWRIGHT: No.

(They're still asleep.)

No.

(They don't wake up.)

Excuse me — I said no!

(Nothing.)

NO! Wake up!

(Crosses to He and She.)

I SAID WAKE UP!!!!

HE: *(They wake up. To the Playwright.)* I was in the middle of a nice dream — making lingerie for my grandmother.

SHE: I dreamt that I had a lithp *(Translation: I dreamt that I had a lisp.)*.

HE: You do.

SHE: Oh.

HE: Hey, I was also narcoleptic in my dream.

SHE: Tho wath I! *(Translation: So was I.)*

(He and She instantly fall asleep.)

PLAYWRIGHT: Excuse me — I'm trying to talk to you. Wake up!

HE: *(They wake up. To the Playwright.)* I was in the middle of a nice dream about being in the middle of a nice dream — making lingerie for my grandmother.

SHE: I dreamt that I dreamt that I had a lithp *(Translation: I dreamt that I dreamt that I had a lisp.)*.

HE: You do.

SHE: Oh.

HE: Hey, I was also narcoleptic in my dream.

SHE: Tho wath I! *(Translation: So was I.)*

PLAYWRIGHT: Don't fall asleep!

HE: I won't — you have my word. *(Beat. He instantly falls asleep.)*

PLAYWRIGHT: Please — listen to me.

SHE: You have my undivided attenthion. *(Translation: You have my undivided attention.)*

(Beat. She instantly falls asleep.)

PLAYWRIGHT: *(Stands on desk chair, commanding attention.)* I DEMAND YOU WAKE UP!

HE: *(Wakes up. To the Playwright.)* I was in the middle of a nice dream about being in the middle of a nice dream about being in the middle of a nice dream — making lingerie for my grandmother.

SHE: I dreamt that I dreamt that I dreamt that I had a lithp. *(Translation: I dreamt that I dreamt that I dreamt that I had a lisp.)*

HE: You do.

SHE: Oh.

PLAYWRIGHT: STOP THIS!

SHE: Thtop what, thilly? *(Translation: Stop what, silly?)*

PLAYWRIGHT: Why are you doing this to me? I'm pouring everything into this — working endlessly to create a simple love story and you have ruined it! Ruined it!

SHE: You made uth thith way. *(Translation: You made us this way.)*

HE: Frankly, it's all wrong.

PLAYWRIGHT: It's my play — my vision!

(Playwright looks out to the audience while He and She instantly fall asleep.)
I must speak to the thousands of lonely people out in this world desperate to find true love. This story needs to be told — our existence as people know it depends upon this play —
(Notices that they have fallen asleep. Falls to the ground begging.)
WILL YOU PLEASE WAKE UP!

HE: *(To the Playwright.)* I was in the middle of a nice dream about —

PLAYWRIGHT: I KNOW — you were making lingerie for your grandmother.

HE: How did you know? This is so embarrassing.

SHE: And I dreamt —

PLAYWRIGHT: *(To She.)* YES — you have a lisp!

SHE: No I don't — thilly. Oopth, I do. *(Translation: No I don't—silly. Oops, I do.)*

HE: The problem is you don't listen to what we want — we have needs. *(Beat.)* You don't get it, do you? Look, briefly putting our narcoleptic tendencies aside, let's say, we were writing the play.
(He and She walk over to the desk.)

PLAYWRIGHT: How absurd!
(She drags the Playwright to the bench to have a seat.)
Noooo!

HE: *(He sits at the desk. Pulling his glasses down a little to look at the computer. He even takes on a very slight English accent.)* Now, I will take your position.

PLAYWRIGHT: But you're not the playwright — you're —

HE: Ah — Ah — Our playwright is mute.

PLAYWRIGHT: *(Angry.)* Mmmmm — mmmmm!
  (Playwright stomps.)

SHE: Our playwright embrathes their muteneth. — *(Translation: Our playwright embraces their muteness.)*

PLAYWRIGHT: *(Playwright embraces self with excitement and enthusiasm.)* Mmmmm. Mmmmm.

SHE: Wait — our playwright talkth with a lithp — like me. *(Translation: Out playwright talks with a lisp — like me.)*

PLAYWRIGHT: I thuddenly have a lithp. *(Translation: I suddenly have a lisp.)*

HE: And wants to share the lisp with the world.

PLAYWRIGHT: I want to thare my lithp with the world! *(Translation: I want to share my lisp with the world.)*

SHE: Playwright realitheth that they knowth nothing about playwriting. *(Translation: Playwright realizes that they knows nothing about playwriting.)*

PLAYWRIGHT: I thuck at writing! And I have a lithp, world! *(Translation: I suck at writing! And I have a lisp, world!)*

HE: Playwright knows nothing about love because the playwright has never been in it.

PLAYWRIGHT: Love ith for foolths! And I have a lithp, world! *(Translation: Love is for fools. And I have a lisp, world!)*

HE: Playwright gives up playwriting.

PLAYWRIGHT: I'm now a pharmathitht! And I have a lithp, world! *(Translation: I'm now a pharmacist! And I have a lisp, world!)*

SHE: Playwright ith narcoleptic. *(Translation: Playwright is narcoleptic.)*

PLAYWRIGHT: I'm narcoleptic! And I have a lithp —
  (Playwright instantly falls asleep and to the ground. "He" stands. He and She have a moment of observation.)

SHE: Nithe perthon. *(Translation: Nice person.)*

HE: *(Without accent.)* Sure was. You know — *(Yawns.)* I'm feeling extremely tired. *(Stretches.)*

SHE: Me too. Maybe we thould go back and thit down. *(Translation: Me too. Maybe we should go back and sit down.)*

HE: Good idea.
  (He yawns. They step over the Playwright and cross to the bench and sit.)
  Now where were we?

SHE: You were thaying that you're narcoleptic. *(He yawns.)* And then I wath thaying that I am altho narcoleptic *(He dozes off to sleep.)* — I mean, ith it pothible two people can meet and find tho much in common? What

if thith ith real love? And you are the one? *(She realizes He's asleep.)* Who knowth, we could be perfect for each other. Thimply thimpatico. *(Translation: You were saying that you're narcoleptic. And then I was saying that I am also narcoleptic — I mean, is it possible two people can meet and find so much in common? What if this is real love? And you are the one. Who knows, we could be perfect for each other. Simply simpatico.)*
(She places his hand in hers then rests her head beside his as lights fade out.)

END OF PLAY

Pistachio Stories

Laura Shamas

For Elizebeth Terzian

CHARACTERS
>RAY: male, thirties.
>MARGUERITE: female, thirties, part Arab-American.
>ROBIN: female, twenties

SETTING
>Major city in United States

TIME
>Now

• • •

Lights come up on Ray, alone on stage.

RAY: I'm being followed around by this red van. No, really, man. Everywhere. Don't call me paranoid. All over the place. You don't believe me? You go look out on the street right now. OK, OK, don't bother. It'll zoom away as soon as you get up to look. And we know why it's following me. Just one reason: because I watch Al-jazeera. Like how else am I supposed to find any real news in this country? It's the only place to find out what's going on. Can't watch BBC 24/7. The press here, they just promote Bush talking points. You know it. I know it. Why watch it? Some people get HBO. Some get Showtime. I get Al-jazeera. And sometimes I have parties to watch Al-jazeera. At my apartment. Yeah. Come all ye Middle East news hounds. I serve hummus, grape leaves, pistachios. Then, believe it or not, we debate issues. Wild times. Back in the day, we called that being a citizen. Anyway, that's when I first see the red van. After the news, I was walking this girl to her car, Marguerite. This girl I know from the area. And I see this red van underneath the street lamp by my apartment. It's big. Glows. All lit up. A nuclear halo around the muffler. I swear, it just radiates. And she sees it, too. And we both think the same thing. But she's smart. She talks in secret code. And she says something about Francis Ford Coppola's movie —
(Light comes up on Marguerite, looking toward the van.)
MARGUERITE: *The Conversation?*
RAY: Yeah. Great flick. Old school.
MARGUERITE: Gene Hackman . . . in there. *(She nods toward the van.)*
RAY: Roger that.

MARGUERITE: How many Arab-Americans does it take to fill an apartment before they bring out the big red van?

(Motor sound starts.)

RAY: Jesus.

MARGUERITE: It's leaving. I scared it.

RAY: *(Shouting.)* We were watching the news! Assholes!

(Lights out on Ray.)

MARGUERITE: But that worried me, that van. I stopped being able to sleep that night. Because I had been telling this other story inside. And now I know the whole thing is on tape or digital or tapped or whatever — this whole thing I said. Christ. And I was talking about the FBI. All innocent, but still, I'm kicking myself. Because Ray, he was serving these red pistachios, and I had to tell him this weird story which happened right after September 11. When we were all terrified. And sad. And Bush tells us to go shopping. That's how he comforts us. That's how he leads us. Because you can never help too many corporations, no matter how much you mourn. You remember when I'm talking about, right? It's September 13, 2001. I'm a grad student. And this girl comes up to me at school. And she says, "Marguerite. You're the only one in the department who can help me. Tell me what this means." And I say, "What, Robin?" And she says:

(Lights up on Robin, carrying books and a backpack.)

ROBIN: I just came from my dad's. They got a strange package. From Syria. And they don't know anyone in Syria. So he opened it. And it's two huge packages of red pistachios. Red pistachios. And there's a note. It says "You know what to do with these. George." So what the hell does that mean? "You know what to do with these. George."

MARGUERITE: How should I know? Who's George?

ROBIN: I don't know. Dad doesn't know. Probably an alias.

MARGUERITE: Well, it must have been a mistake. Wrong delivery. Call the post office.

ROBIN: I think it's a sleeper cell activation signal.

MARGUERITE: A sleeper cell activation signal.

ROBIN: You heard me.

MARGUERITE: Two bags of red pistachios from Syria with a note from George.

ROBIN: "You know what to do with these."

MARGUERITE: He probably meant eat them. It's a delicacy.

ROBIN: A sleeper cell signal that, as luck would have it, went to the wrong address.

MARGUERITE: Or maybe George just wanted his friend to make baklava.

ROBIN: You stand there joking. This could be evidence of a big crime about to happen.

MARGUERITE: If that's what you really think, why don't you go to the FBI? Be a hero, Nancy Drew.

(Robin rummages in her backpack. Hands her two huge bags of red pistachios.)

ROBIN: No. You're going to the FBI. You're Arab-American. You be the hero. Take care of this for the rest of us.

MARGUERITE: No. I don't want these. Robin!!!

ROBIN: *(Backs away.)* After what happened two days ago in New York, it's the least you can do, don't you think? Prove you're more American than Arab. Gotta go. Class in five.

(Robin exits.)

MARGUERITE: *(Tries to catch Robin.)* Come back here, you waspy xenophobic elitist grad school bigot! Robin! *(She looks at the bags.)* So I'm standing there holding these pistachios bags. Racking my brain. Red pistachios. What do they mean? Do I have evidence of a crime in my hands? Should I go to the FBI? How the hell did I get stuck with Robin's nut problem? So I go home, and I Google red pistachios. And I learn how they used to dye green pistachios red in America, because in the early twentieth century, nuts from the Middle East were highly prized. So they dyed nuts from Lebanon, Syria, and Iran red — a sign that they were Middle Eastern. So if you were desperate, you could grow green pistachios in California, dye them red, and claim they were from the Middle East. But, but there were places in Syria where a special red pistachio nut tree really grows. It's not fake. And I think to myself, isn't that what George's giving to his friend? A true taste of the Middle East? Not this fake stuff. The real deal. The red nuts were so good that the Romans took 'em back to Italy for emperors. Two bags of red pistachios from Syria say: "Special. Blood. Of the earth." I'm pissed as hell at Robin. I don't know what to do with the stray nuts. I take them home, put them on a shelf. I stare at them every night. I weigh the pros and cons of going to the FBI. On one hand, they could say, "Thanks and why are you giving us these nuts? The package wasn't addressed to you. That's a federal offense, opening someone else's mail. We're locking you up." You know Robin would deny the truth. Hell, maybe she's setting me up! Or they could say, "Oh, you weren't in our files before but thanks for making us aware of you, weird nut lady. We're going to watch you like a hawk from now on, you Arab-American woman in your reproductive years who reports random Syrian pistachio deliveries." So I keep staring at the nuts for two weeks. Cursing Robin.

Until finally, I think, you know, they look pretty good. Would it hurt if I ate . . . just one? Shouldn't I eat a kernel? I can still turn the bags in if I need to, with just one nut missing." So I open one bag.

(She opens it. She eats one and savors it.)

And it's so good, this red pistachio from Syria. So I eat another one. And another one. One week later, the whole first bag is gone and I'm onto the next. And I'm so happy. I am eating red pistachios from Syria. And I call my mom. And she has this great recipe for Sitti's baklava. And I make it. And I eat it. And I've gained four pounds by the end of the second bag. And maybe, just maybe, George, whoever he is, would be happy. So this is the story I've been telling at Ray's apartment as we're watching Aljazeera. And then when I leave, I realize that the whole stinking thing has been recorded by the red van. And I don't sleep well after that. But when I see him the next week, Ray says not to worry.

(Lights come up again on Ray, wearing a different shirt. Marguerite puts on a light jacket as they talk.)

RAY: That nut story. It's cute. What can they do? That was years ago. There's been no terrorist sleep cell awakened on U.S. soil.

MARGUERITE: Not yet. But what if there is some day? And what if there's some Arab red nut involvement?

RAY: *(Patting her shoulders.)* Your story reminds me, I have this friend Rochelle. She just got back from Beirut. She hadn't been for twenty-five years, but her aunt was dying, and she went. She had the best time, even though her aunt passed as soon as she got back here. She feels everywhere she went, there were people who connected with her, who appreciated her. She felt good speaking Arabic. She fit in. And their four kids are grown now, so she and her husband, they might move back. She has a round red mark, right here, on her face.

(Ray points to his lower left cheek of his face.)

MARGUERITE: How big?

RAY: As big as a dime. And everyone here, they tell her to get plastic surgery, to get it removed. They say, "Zap that birthmark. Get it lasered."

MARGUERITE: "Get it airbrushed. Get it Photoshopped. Cover it with make-up."

RAY: But she won't. Rochelle tells this story. When she was a young girl, Rochelle asked her mother about the red mark. And her mother said that before Rochelle was born, while her mom was pregnant, she'd eaten red pistachios in a grove on a hill. And Rochelle's so special to have a red pistachio mark. A gift from God. The mark is a tie to her mother's pregnancy and to Lebanon. Rochelle thinks it's another reason to move back to the Middle East. A sign.

MARGUERITE: *(A pause.)* Sitti says you throw pistachios in weddings to give long life to the bride and groom.

RAY: You never gave them to travelers as good luck? Another old custom. That could be why this George sent them to his friend. A bon voyage present. As simple as that.

MARGUERITE: Your friend Rochelle's brave.

RAY: So see you next week for the weekly Al-jazeera truth hit?

(She turns to look at him.)

MARGUERITE: Ray, I don't think I can come anymore.

RAY: Why not?

MARGUERITE: Because . . . what good does it do? So we see the real news? So we know the real Middle East. So what.

RAY: How else will we live through these times? We have to remember some-how.

MARGUERITE: No. No. Maybe it's time we forget.

(Motor sounds again. Lights out on Marguerite.)

RAY: And Marguerite goes home. She never came to watch the news with me again. I see the red van pull away, in the shadows. I see it when I leave work. I see it at the grocery. I see it at the gas station. I see it at the bank. I hear funny scratches on my phone line, when I'm talking to my cousins. They are following me. You think I'm paranoid. I know you do. But the truth is, they are following you, too. You watch. You'll see a red van. You'll say something innocent — you'll be talking about your family, or mem-ories, or weddings, or funerals, or pistachios. Then you'll see a red van. And your heart will sink.

(Blackout.)

END OF PLAY

The Searcher

FREDERICK STROPPEL

CHARACTERS

    ANNETTE

    HARLEY

    TONY

SETTING

    A living room

• • •

The living room of a lower-middle-class home. There is a vigorous knocking at the door. Annette, in her late forties, enters.

ANNETTE: Coming, coming, don't get your hair in a braid.
    (Answers the door.)
    Yes?
    (Harley, in his twenties, enters.)

HARLEY: Mrs. Mancuso?

ANNETTE: Yes?

HARLEY: *(Checks a piece of paper.)* Annette Mancuso?

ANNETTE: Yes?

HARLEY: Mom?

ANNETTE: *(Bewildered.)* Mom?

HARLEY: It's me — Harley. Your son!

ANNETTE: My son?
    (Harley throws himself at her, gives her a big hug.)
    Oof!

HARLEY: Mom! Mommy! I can't believe I found you!

ANNETTE: I think there may be a mistake . . .

HARLEY: I know, it's a shock, isn't it, after all these years? Maybe I should have called first, but I wanted to see the look on your face.
    (She looks quite stupefied.)
    Yes, this is worth all the months and months of searching, tracking down false leads, stumbling down blind alleys, turning over every rock I could find . . .

ANNETTE: Listen, young man . . .

HARLEY: Harley. My other parents renamed me Wallace — Wallace, can you believe that? — but now I've gone back to the name that you gave me — Harley Mancuso. And I say it with pride.

ANNETTE: I didn't give you any name. I don't know who you are.

HARLEY: I'm your son. Geez, Mom, I know I was only nine months old when you gave me up for adoption, but still, you ought to be able to recognize flesh of your flesh, blood of your blood. I've still got that birthmark. Look. *(Harley turns around and lowers his pants.)*

ANNETTE: *(Turns away.)* Oh, dear . . . !

HARLEY: I shaved away all the surrounding hair so you could get a good look. See, it's like a swastika.

ANNETTE: Please pull your pants up. My husband's in the next room.

HARLEY: *(Pulls up his pants.)* I can't wait to meet him. Now is he my real dad?

ANNETTE: No, he's not your real dad. Because I'm not your real mom!

HARLEY: Mom, please, you don't have to maintain this charade for my sake. Can't you imagine how exciting this moment is for me — coming face-to-face with the very source of my existence? I mean, these are the lips that first kissed me.
(Points to her breasts.)
And this is where I first found nourishment . . .
(Points to her crotch.)
And down there is where I first entered the world . . .

ANNETTE: Before you finish the grand tour, let's get something straight: I don't know what the hell you're talking about. You're not my child. I've never had a child.

HARLEY: I can see how you might feel that way. But I don't blame you for abandoning me. You were young, you were foolish. You were driven by personal demons, probably drug-induced. You may have sold your body a couple of times to make ends meet.

ANNETTE: Where did you hear about that?

HARLEY: It's all right, Mom, I understand. You've led a luckless hardscrabble life, your face is pinched and worn, you're old beyond your years. But that phase of your life is over. My trust fund has matured, and I now have the means to lift you out of this sordid white-trash hell hole and give you the comfortable life you deserve.

ANNETTE: You have a trust fund?

HARLEY: As you know, my adoptive parents were pretty well off. I've never wanted for anything: the best schools, the nicest clothes, the fanciest cars — all thanks to you, Mom; and now it's my turn to give something back.

ANNETTE: *(As if recognizing.)* Harley! Of course! Sit down, son.

HARLEY: *(Declines.)* I couldn't possibly sit, I have too much nervous energy. This is like a dream come true. You know, I never knew the truth about my parentage until I was out of college. One night the mater and pater came home from the club with a couple of cocktails under their belts, and they started sniping at each other, as drunken couples will, and Mom called Dad "a dried-up old ball sac" — just in a joshing sense, of course, but the moment I heard it, everything clicked into place. I suddenly knew that I was living a lie, and that nothing would be right with me until I reconnected with the woman who carried me in her womb and flushed me into the world on a river of her own blood.

ANNETTE: That's sweet. So were you thinking a series of payments spread out over a number of years, or just one big check to cover everything?

HARLEY: We have all the time in the world to figure that out. First, I'm taking you to dinner. Have you been to the Villa Pierre?

ANNETTE: That's so expensive! Let me get my coat.

(She heads off to get it.)

HARLEY: It seems funny now, looking back at all the rigmarole I went through to find you. Poring endlessly through the Internet, hiring private detectives . . . And it all started with that misprint on the adoption record, which got me off on the wrong track from the get-go.

ANNETTE: *(Pulling on her coat.)* Misprint?

HARLEY: Yes, the clerk or someone wrote down Antoinette instead of Annette. Sloppy and inexcusable.

ANNETTE: *(Troubled.)* Antoinette . . . ?

HARLEY: I was spinning my wheels for a good six months, looking for some nonexistent woman. If it hadn't been for my own persistence and the guidance of a Higher Power, I never would have found you.

ANNETTE: *(Now realizing.)* Oh . . . you're Harley.

HARLEY: Yes . . . ?

ANNETTE: Oh dear . . . I think . . . just a minute . . .

(Yells into the next room.)

Tony!

(Tony walks out — middle-aged, beer belly, a grizzly beard.)

TONY: Yeah?

ANNETTE: This young man here . . .

(Tony stops dead in his tracks.)

TONY: Harley . . . ?

HARLEY: Huh?

(Tony moves forward, stares at Harley, stunned.)

TONY: Harley? Is it really you? Well, I'll be a son of a bitch! Why, the last time I saw you, you were still shitting yellow — and now look at you: all grown up! Come to me, son! Come to me!

(He wraps his arms around Harley in a bear hug.)

HARLEY: Son? You mean — you're my father?

TONY: No — I'm your mother.

HARLEY: My . . . what?

TONY: I'm your mom!

HARLEY: I'm not . . . understanding this . . .

TONY: Well, you see, Harley, I've been on something of a personal journey. With many twists and turns along the way. But enough about me. Whatcha been up to, boy? You still got that birthmark? Let me see.

HARLEY: No, I don't . . .

TONY: *(Yanking at his pants.)* Oh come on. You're not gonna be bashful with me.

(Harley manages to get away from him.)

HARLEY: *(Eluding him.)* Dad — Mom — I need a moment to get my head around this. You were a woman, and now . . . ?

TONY: I'm all man. Right, Sugar buns?

(He gives Annette a playful swat on the behind.)

ANNETTE: Ow! Tony, not in front of . . .

TONY: Oh, he's family.

HARLEY: So you, what — had surgery?

TONY: The whole nine yards. Wanna take a look?

(Starts to unzip his pants.)

HARLEY: No . . . !

TONY: He's a shy one, isn't he?

ANNETTE: He's got some money for us.

TONY: Shit, I don't need any money. I've got my son back, that's all that matters.

ANNETTE: Don't talk foolish now, Tony.

HARLEY: I'm still at a bit of a loss here. You had an operation, and now you're a man, but you were a woman when you had me . . . ?

TONY: Well, of course I was a woman. That's simple biology, isn't it?

HARLEY: But what happened? You had some kind of gender crisis, or something . . . ?

TONY: Well, I guess I always knew, deep down. As a child I was quite the tomboy. Played a lot of field hockey. Wasn't much for wearing dresses. Didn't have the legs for them, anyway.

ANNETTE: Oh, you have beautiful legs.

TONY: As I grew older, I tried to be more ladylike. Went through a whole *Cosmopolitan* phase. And had my share of romantic entanglements, obviously. But my mind and my body were at cross-purposes. I was living a lie.

ANNETTE: *(To Harley.)* Oh — just like you.

TONY: It was time to make a real commitment. And as the Good Lord would have it, I crossed paths with a childless couple from the upper tenth percentile. They wanted a baby, and I wanted some reconstructive surgery. And the money was right. Do you blame me, son?

(Getting emotional.)

It's not like I wanted to get rid of you. Because if there was any way . . . I mean, you were my son, Goddamit . . . !

(Tony starts crying, and turns away.)

ANNETTE: Don't mind the crying. He's still got a few of the old hormones in him. You should have seen him bawling when they voted the blind girl off *American Idol*.

TONY: That was a bullshit vote!

ANNETTE: She was off-key, honey. And she had a real attitude.

TONY: She was fucking blind! The cold-hearted bastards!

ANNETTE: All right, let's not revisit this topic again. Who's for coffee?

HARLEY: I'd like a drink, if you don't mind.

TONY: *(Cheers up.)* That's my boy. Get us a coupla Meisterbraus, and see if there's any of that Captain Morgan left. I mighta killed it last night.

(Annette exits.)

She's good people. We were in the same grade school together — used to jump rope in the playground. Funny how things turn out.

HARLEY: *(Sits down beside Tony.)* So what about my father? Was his name Harley?

TONY: Well, I'm not exactly sure what his name was.

HARLEY: You didn't know him?

TONY: Of course I knew him. You think I'm some kind of slut? I just don't have all the particulars. But I'm pretty sure he was a biker.

HARLEY: A biker?

TONY: He belonged to a fraternal organization called the Golden Guineas. That was how we probably met. I had a thing for bikes, myself, and I wanted to join the gang. And as part of the initiation, they sort of passed me around.

HARLEY: *(Gasps.)* You were gang-raped?

TONY: No, no. My, the ideas you young people have. No, we went to a motel, and they all took turns like gentlemen. There were never more than three people in the room at a time. But those were free-wheeling times, nobody thought much about using condoms or even washing up afterwards, so I wound up in the family way. In a sense, they were all your fathers. And a grander bunch of guys you couldn't hope to meet.

HARLEY: So you were a single mother? You had to pay all the hospital bills yourself?

TONY: *(Scoffs.)* Hospital? I wish. No, son, you were born the natural way, under a bypass off Route 29. I had to yank you out myself. That's why you've got those jug ears. Ah, memories.

HARLEY: *(Writing in a pad.)* "The Golden Guineas . . ." Maybe I can Google them.

TONY: The gang's probably broken up by now, not likely you'll find anybody. *(Narrows his eyes.)*

Now that I look at you, though, damned if you ain't the spitting image of Willie Possum.

HARLEY: Willie Possum?

TONY: He was a crazy man. When I met him, he'd just gotten out of jail — tried to blow up City Hall, you know — and he was a man on a mission. We must have gone at it for four hours straight — backwards, sideways, against the wall . . . Well, that's neither here nor there. But black out a couple of your teeth, you could be his twin.

(Annette returns with the beers.)

TONY: What do you think, hon? Willie Possum?

ANNETTE: *(Looks at Harley.)* Jesus Christ, yes.

(Surprised.)

I didn't know you slept with him.

TONY: Well, I'm not gonna tell you everything.

HARLEY: So, do you keep in touch with Mr. Possum?

TONY: *(Chuckles.)* No, he's pretty much dead nowadays. Got into a knife fight at the county fair back in '93, and wound up stabbing himself. What a character.

ANNETTE: Better hope you don't get too many of his genes.

TONY: *(Looks at Harley proudly.)* No, he's a Mancuso, through and through. *(Arm around Harley's neck.)*

Speaking of which, how's your love life? Are you getting laid?

ANNETTE: Tony, please — that's not something he's going to tell his mother.

TONY: Just taking an interest.

HARLEY: I don't have any girlfriends at the moment.

TONY: Aha . . .

HARLEY: No, it's not that. I just haven't met the right person . . .

(Tony and Annette nod knowingly.)

ANNETTE: A chip off the old block.

TONY: *(Points to Harley's crotch.)* Let me know if you don't have any use for that thing; I don't mind tacking on a few extra inches.

(Laughs.)

Just breaking your chops. You're still young, you have plenty of time to figure out what the fuck you are.

HARLEY: *(Backing away.)* Well, Mom, it's been nice touching base with you, but I gotta be on my way . . .

TONY: Where are you going? You're having dinner with us. We just got a fresh bucket from the Colonel.

ANNETTE: No, all their fryers were down. I had to get the premade sandwiches from the Super-Seven. But anyway, he's taking us to a fancy restaurant.

HARLEY: I'm not sure if that's a great idea . . .

TONY: Yeah, I don't feel like changing my shirt again. I got a better idea. There's a place down on River Road, called Rudy's Beefalo, where all the guys hang out. We can grab some cheese steaks and onion straws, just the two of us, my treat. Best corn dogs in town. What do you say?

HARLEY: I'm not really in the mood.

TONY: Oh, now, don't be such a grumpy-pants. I know how to put a smile on your face.

(Tony tickles his chin, and makes faces and baby sounds.)

Gubba-goobba-geebbee . . . !

HARLEY: *(Not smiling.)* Look, Mom, I just don't think we should be seen in public together.

TONY: Why not? What's the matter?

(Realizes.)

You're ashamed of me, aren't you?

HARLEY: No . . .

TONY: I'm not rich and glamorous like your other mother.

HARLEY: It's not that . . .

TONY: Sure, I'm just an ordinary working stiff. My hands are rough, not smooth and silky. I guess I must be a pretty big disappointment to you.

HARLEY: "Disappointment" isn't really the word. I just need a little distance right now. I'll come back some other day, we can play golf or something.

TONY: Golf is for pussies . . . !

(Grudgingly.)

Yeah, sure, that would be a blast.

ANNETTE: It was good of you to come, Harley. We'll look forward to seeing you again, and working out that whole money thing.

(Harley nods, heads for the door.)

TONY: Before you go — can I just see the birthmark?

HARLEY: Mom . . .

TONY: Please. It would mean so much.

(Harley relents. He turns around and lowers his pants.)

TONY: Jesus, that is one hairless ass.

ANNETTE: He shaved it.

TONY: Shaved it? What kind of weird shit are you into?

HARLEY: Will you just look at the fucking birthmark?

TONY: (Spots the birthmark.) There it is — Just like a little spider . . .

(Starts to cry, wiping his eyes.)

Fucking hormones . . . !

(Tony sits down, weepy, as Harley pulls up his pants.)

ANNETTE: (Gently.) Go to your mom. She needs you.

(Harley pats Tony's shoulder.)

HARLEY: It's OK, Mom, it's OK . . .

TONY: I never should have let you go! All the wasted years, the time we could have had together . . . !

HARLEY: Well, we're together now.

(Tony, overcome by emotions, pulls Harley close and buries his weeping face in his son's abdomen. Harley endures the moment as best he can. Beat.)

HARLEY: Tell you what, Mom — let's you and me go to the Beefalo.

TONY: You mean it?

HARLEY: But I'm buying.

TONY: I'll get the helmets.

HARLEY: Helmets?

(Tony heads out.)

ANNETTE: Don't worry, Harley. With the passage of time, it all starts to seem normal.

HARLEY: Did you know when you married him?

ANNETTE: He looked familiar, but I never made the connection. Still, I have no complaints.

(A little smile.)

Confidentially, I'm into some weird shit myself.

(She gives him a very creepy look.)

(Tony returns wearing a motorcycle helmet, and carrying a second one for Harley.)

TONY: OK, saddle up.

HARLEY: But — I can't drive a motorcycle.

TONY: You're riding shotgun with me, sonny boy.

(Tony puts the helmet on Harley's head.)

Tuck those ears in . . .

ANNETTE: So cute! Let me get the camera.

TONY: *(Seriously.)* Now, look — at the Beefalo, we're just cycle buddies, OK? Some of those boys wouldn't understand.

HARLEY: I'm not going to say a word.

ANNETTE: *(Aiming a disposable camera.)* OK, smile!

(Harley can't quite muster a smile. So Tony tickles him under the chin.)

TONY: Gubba-goobba-geebbee!

(Now Harley smiles.)

TONY: That's my boy!

(They pose, and Annette snaps the picture.)
(Blackout.)

END OF PLAY

More

Jeff Tabnick

CHARACTERS
    ROB: male, late twenties
    VAL: female, late twenties
    STEVE: male, late twenties

SETTING
    Living room

TIME
    Present

• • •

Living room. Television, couch, etc. Val sits languidly on the couch. Rob paces, holding a videotape. A knock at the door. Rob hurries to the door and opens it up. Val stays seated.

ROB: Thanks so much for coming to see us again. And sorry about the unpleasantness last time.

VAL: *(Overlapping at "unpleasantness.")* It was a bad idea.

ROB: It didn't seem that way at the time.

VAL: It was a very bad idea.

ROB: We were desperate. Come in, come in.
    (Steve hesitantly enters. He's good-looking and easy-going.)

ROB: Good to see you, thank you so much.
    (Steve just nods his head good-naturedly. He looks at Val and grins. Val looks away.)

STEVE: Sorry.

VAL: Every time I think about it I — I have to emit a little noise. Just to make the thought of it go away —.
    (Val emits a little noise.)

ROB: But that's in the past . . .

STEVE: *(Overlapping on "past.")* I'm not like —

ROB: . . . right?

STEVE: — um, sure —
    (Returning to his thought.)
    — I'm not a doctor or anything.
    (Val stops emitting the noise.)

ROB: Of course you're not.

STEVE: I'm a bartender.

ROB: You're my friend.

STEVE: I'm you're bartender.

ROB: We talk a lot.

STEVE: Sure we do because I'm you're —

ROB: A lot.

STEVE: At the bar you go to.

ROB: And I know about you, you fucking dog. You dog you . . .

> *(To Val, trying to impress her.)*

He gets it at least once a week —

VAL: You've told me.

ROB: *(Continuous.)* I'm drinking, my jaw drops. He gets it all the time.

VAL: You've told me.

ROB: *(Continuous.)* With the girls at the bar. You fucking dog. His numbers must be. Through the roof.

STEVE: Right which is why you had me over last week? Which is why you thought it would be ok —

ROB: That wasn't the intention going into it.

> *(Val struggles to not emit the noise.)*

STEVE: I thought maybe we were going to have a threesome.

ROB: Well . . .

VAL: We were never going to have a threesome.

ROB: Never.

STEVE: I come in, you two tell me you want me to watch you have sex so I jumped right in . . .

> *(Val emits the noise.)*

STEVE: . . . what was I supposed to think.

ROB: We just wanted you to *watch*. So this time . . . .

> *(Val stops emitting the noise.)*
> *(Rob puts the tape in the VCR and fiddles with the VCR during the following dialogue.)*

STEVE: The clinical thing is not really my bag.

> *(Steve sits on the couch next to Val.)*

STEVE: *(To Val.)* Do you think there's a problem?

ROB: . . . this time . . .

VAL: He wants this; if this goes OK, he'll give me something I want.

STEVE: Maybe the problem isn't *that*.

VAL: You think there's a problem other than maybe that?

> *(Rob gets up from the VCR, remote control in his hand.)*

ROB: This time you'll watch us have sex on tape!

STEVE: No. Normal. Everything's very normal.

(Rob stands behind the couch and hits play on the remote and the video starts. There should be no sound on the video. If we see anything, we see the flickering light on their faces.)

STEVE: OK. Oh. OK.

(Val starts to emit the noise.)

ROB: Stop that.

(Val stops emitting the noise.)

ROB: You see, Steve, all that other stuff, other problems we may or may not have. We can figure that out. We see other people bickering or manipulating or deceiving or reconciling out in public. Or in the movies. We see people having babies and raising kids on TV. What we don't see in public or in the movies or on TV is this. Except for porn but that's not what we're trying to get at. These private things. How do you know if you're doing them right. If they're private. For everyone.

STEVE: Right.

ROB: Like wiping your ass.

VAL: Rob!

ROB: What? I'm just — How does anyone know if he's wiping his ass the right way, the optimum way?

VAL: I resent that analogy.

ROB: Have you ever seen anyone else do it?

STEVE: You want an objective opinion.

VAL: You could tell me I should care about homeless people or you could tell me I should care about Rob and I having good sex. They both sound like absurd things to care about to me.

ROB: Right. But. And this precisely is the problem.

STEVE: So . . . no foreplay.

VAL: No we do foreplay.

ROB: We do but —

VAL: It's really the act of sex —

ROB: Right, well it's not a question of do we enjoy it, sure we do.

VAL: I get off.

ROB: See this precisely is the problem.

STEVE: What is it you want me to judge?

ROB: Is it doing what it's supposed to do.

STEVE: Is it doing what it's supposed to do?

ROB: A hand job is just about getting off but sex isn't sex supposed to be about something more?

STEVE: Is it?

VAL: I don't know.

ROB: I need to know if we have this more.

STEVE: *(To Val.)* Are you experiencing this more?

VAL: I can't talk about.

ROB: If she could we wouldn't be showing you a tape of us going at it.

VAL: *(Intentionally.)* I'm not good orally, I mean verbally.

STEVE: There's supposed to be more?

> *(Steve, suddenly interested, leans into the TV.)*

ROB: In relationships, don't you think? You see something?

STEVE: I'm looking for this "more" . . .

ROB: Do you see it?

STEVE: . . . this "more" than just getting off. I thought it was a myth.

ROB: Something to give it some weight. Some meaning. Before I really commit, I need to know if we have that.

STEVE: You look. Intense.

ROB: I'm trying to connect. Do you think she should be looking at me more, maybe she should be looking at me more.

> *(The dialogue in boldface should be more prominent.)*

ROB: *(To Steve.)* **Should I be going at her harder, more virile, or should I back off some.** More gentle. **See she doesn't look at me.**

STEVE: It does feel like masturbation a lot. For me. Maybe it's this more that I've been missing.

I remember when I was a kid. I used to whack off all the time. On all sorts of textures. Whatever.

VAL: I need to concentrate.

ROB: On what, because it sure ain't me. Maybe the connection comes out is of the animalness of it, or maybe the tenderness? **Don't you think the effect is muddy?**

And I thought man I hope sex is better than masturbation. But how would it be?

Maybe she shoots something inside of me! This is what I thought.

VAL: **I get off.**

STEVE: But it didn't take me long to figure out that she doesn't shoot anything inside of me. With the right damp washrag, sex was just like masturbation. With really good porno.

ROB: But look, you see in a relationship I think it should be, different.

STEVE: That's what I'm looking for. This more.

ROB: For the substance. Do you see the substance?

(Rob joins the others on the couch and the three look at the TV intently for a few moments, trying to find this substance, this more.)

ROB: Proof of more going on, proof of more.

(Steve leans into the TV and looks at it very very hard, still trying to decipher something. Then after a few moments . . .)

STEVE: Um. Well. I can say this. It's good form. The act is well formed. And I've seen a lot of that form in my time, Val, and your form is good.

ROB: But the — what about the — ?

(Beat.)

Huh. The form's good? You really think that?

STEVE: Yeah.

ROB: And her form?

STEVE: Oh yeah. You've got it pretty good having her.

ROB: I got it pretty good having her, huh? Having that?

STEVE: Yeah.

VAL: Rob!

ROB: I didn't mean that like an . . .

(They watch the big finish. Rob looks more pleased. Steve tries once again to decipher something from it. Val looks away and can't help emitting the noise.)

STEVE: And that's an end.

(Val stops emitting the noise.)

ROB: I was nervous, with the camera.

VAL: I did get off. I always do.

ROB: That's right and so did I.

ROB AND VAL: Almost at the same time.

(Val smiles weakly at Rob.)

VAL: *(Trying to be kind.)* Maybe that means there's something deeper under it. A connection.

(Giving up on kindness, settling for honesty.)

Or we just know each other's bodies.

(Rob turns the TV off and smiles to himself.)

STEVE: I'm very glad I've watched this.

VAL: I'm sure.

STEVE: *(Despondent but convincing himself otherwise.)* I was always worried that maybe I was missing something by not having relationship sex. Missing that thing that makes sex better. But I can't see any proof of that here. Looks the same as all the single sex I have. No proof of connection. Getting off. But I get to get off with more people. Good for me. Ha! Good night, I've gotta get to work.

(Steve leaves.)

VAL: That was inconclusive.

ROB: He did say it was good form.

VAL: But what about all that other stuff, the weight, the connection, the substance, the more . . .

ROB: Obviously unprovable. So. Good form. That's not easy to come by either. I'll take it.

VAL: Good. I gave you what you want?

ROB: Yes.

VAL: So now you give me what I want.
(Rob sits next to her and kisses her.)

ROB: One baby. Coming up.
(They start going at it.)
(Blackout.)

END OF PLAY

Weird Water

Robert Lewis Vaughan

This play is for Bonnie Metzgar and Chip Walton.
Special thanks to Aaron Clayton, Dee Covington, and Austin Pendleton; and
special thanks to Drew DeCorletto and Leo Lauer of Broken Watch Theatre
Company for the use of the Michael Weller Theatre.

CHARACTERS

> HAL: fifties, Tommy's Father
> LIBBY: fifties, Tommy's Mother
> JEFF: twenty-five, Tommy's best friend

SETTING

> Tommy's bedroom

• • •

Black. Silence. Dim light from downstairs comes up and we see a man, Hal, sitting on Tommy's bed. Hal flicks a remote and turns on a television set — the soft glow brightens the room. We hear a reporter's voice —

MALE REPORTER: Returning to the White House two days early from vacation at his ranch in Crawford, Texas, the president said today the United States would —

> *(Hal flicks the remote, changes the channel.)*

FEMALE REPORTER: When interviewed from his ranch in Crawford, Texas, about the most recent attacks the president said —

> *(Hal flicks the remote again.)*

ANNOUNCER: This Is CNN.

> *(Again.)*

LOCAL NEWS REPORTER: Reporting from Crawford, this is John Jenson for KXIT in Amarillo, the Panhandle's News Leader —

> *(Hal turns off the power to the set. Tommy's room is dark again. A moment. A hallway light comes on. Libby appears in the doorway to the bedroom. She reaches into the room and feels for the light switch. A small bedside lamp comes on. Hal remains sitting on the bed. Libby stands in the doorway. She looks at him. He does not look at her. A moment.)*

HAL: Why the hell do you think he had this small, lamp with a dim bulb connected to the light switch instead of the bright desk lamp? Can't see anything.

> *(She does not leave the doorway.)*

LIBBY: You were sittin' in the dark anyway. What could you see? . . . How long have you been in here today?

HAL: I think that little lamp could probably stand a bulb with a higher wattage, don't you? What do you think he has in there anyway? Twenty-five watts? Think it could stand a sixty?

LIBBY: They had Darcy's birthday party at the office today. Sue brought those cookies she made for the Christmas party last year.

(He turns the TV back on and surfs.)

Didn't you say you liked those cookies? I know you said you liked those cookies. She always makes more than she needs to. I brought some home. You remember likin' those cookies? I think I finally talked her into givin' me the dad-gum recipe.

HAL: He programmed every news network into this favorite channel button. The History Channel. Didn't he used to call that the "Hitler Channel"? The Discovery Channel. MTV. VH1. And the Golf Channel. I didn't even know there was a Golf Channel. Did you know there was Golf Channel?

(He flicks off the television.)

I didn't know he liked golf so much that he'd set the Golf Channel this way? Did you know he liked golf that much?

LIBBY: . . . They're the cookies with the —

(He flicks the remote and the television is back on.)

HAL: Look at this, would you? There's a Goddamned Golf Channel.

(The golf commentator's sotto voce ramblings are coming from the TV.)

LIBBY: How long have you been sitting up here today?

HAL: You home early or somethin'?

LIBBY: It's six thirty. Didn't you even notice you were sitting in the dark? That the sun went down? Again?

(He switches channels.)

Come on back downstairs with me Hal. There's somebody —

HAL: Why don't your feet don't step across the line from the gray carpet in the hallway to the blue carpet in here? Blue. Gray — in your own son's Goddamn room.

LIBBY: Jeff's downstairs.

HAL: How long, Libby?

LIBBY: How long what? . . . Have you been sittin' in here in the dark?

HAL: Since you came into this room?

LIBBY: You spend enough time in here for both us.

(He changes channels again and she reaches back inside, flips the switch off, and walks away leaving him in the dark — except for the glow from the TV screen and the faint light from the hallway. He surfs. A moment.)

HAL: . . . Goddamn Golf Channel.

(A moment. A young man walks into the light and stops at the doorway to the bedroom. He's framed in the light from the hall. He's holding a plate of cookies. The young man, Jeff, says nothing and Hal doesn't notice him. Hal surfs again and stops on MTV.)

MTV: Welcome back to MTV's Choose or Lose Special.

(Hal surfs.)

JEFF: Libby said if I was gonna come on up here to see you I should bring these cookies.

(Jeff steps into the room and turns on the desk lamp. He leans on the desk but does not sit.)

HAL: What're you doing here, Jeff? I thought you moved to Austin —

JEFF: I came up for the weekend. See Mama and them . . .

HAL: Nice of you.

JEFF: Family thing — 'cause . . . I got engaged. Lisa — she . . . Tommy . . . She . . .

HAL: I remember Libby saying something about the little gal you were with at . . .

JEFF: I guess his funeral was the last time I saw you. Huh?

HAL: You and Tommy went off to school. And you stayed . . . in school. You stayed here. You finished up and you're building a life for yourself. Now you're planning to —

JEFF: Next spring.

HAL: Your mama and daddy must be real proud of you.

JEFF: Mama's just goin' crazy and . . .

(Pause.)

I'm not gonna have a best man.

HAL: Now why would you go sayin' somethin' like that?

JEFF: He was my best friend since we were what? Six? When we moved in over here across the street? Tommy's my Best Man, Hal — nobody else is gonna stand where he shouldda been standin'.

(Silence.)

Libby said you been stayin' up here a lot.

HAL: Where he shouldda been standin' . . . yes, sir. You might want to write yourself a letter to the drunk driver responsible for that. Yes, sir, you might want to let that man know how you feel about things.

JEFF: Hal . . .

HAL: Did you know Tommy had the Golf Channel programmed into this thing, here?

JEFF: I wanted to talk to you more at his funeral. I meant to . . . I never . . . I didn't know how. I didn't know what to say.

HAL: I don't know what to say either. I still just don't know what to say. You tried them cookies, Jeff?

JEFF: I tried to talk him out of it. I wanted him to stay in school with me.

HAL: Libby tried to talk him out of it too.

JEFF: He made up his own mind.

HAL: That's what I taught my son to do . . . make up his own mind.

JEFF: He loved you so much for that. I wish me and my dad — we —

HAL: Y'all used to butt heads. You two getting' along any better?

JEFF: Well. He's always gonna wanna tell me how to do things. He still doesn't listen to what I have to say —

HAL: Runnin' a business — he's runnin' a business, Jeff. Everybody's gotta run a business. Maybe I shouldda —

JEFF: How's the store doin'?

HAL: Jerry's my right hand down there — don't know what I'd do without him. People're always gonna need trophies. Schools — businesses — all the social clubs. And . . . World's Best Moms . . . World's Best Dads . . .

JEFF: My old man's still . . . I always envied Tommy and you. Did you know that? Did Tommy ever say anything to you about that?

HAL: Not a thing.

JEFF: Well, maybe it was —

HAL: Your daddy tried to teach you everything he knew. Didn't he? He has a strong will and strong beliefs — and he wanted you to . . .

JEFF: You did that with Tommy —

HAL: Libby and I never — we taught Tommy to think for himself. We didn't think we should . . . spoon-feed him. We wanted him to ask questions.

JEFF: And he did. All the time. About everything.

HAL: I didn't tell him he shouldn't join the army.

JEFF: Why?

(Pause.)

Why didn't you try to talk him out of it, Hal? He'd've listen to you. I know he'd've listened to you.

HAL: And I feel like I helped murder my son.

JEFF: — Hal. I didn't mean —

HAL: It's a game. That's all it is, Jeff — a playground game. Follow the leader. But who in the hell was he followin'?

JEFF: It's because of Pat Tillman. When he heard what Tillman did? That he got killed — it's . . . that's what it was. That guy gave up millions and walked away from his football career: Tommy thought that was unbelievable — it was all over the news. The interviews. Why he gave it up to join and . . . by the time people found out about what really happened to Tillman — it was too late. Wasn't it? For Tommy.

HAL: He knew I had serious doubts about what the hell we were doing over there. He didn't ask me any questions about that though. I didn't try to explain myself to him. Diving in like that — I should have put my foot down.

JEFF: He wouldda done it anyway. When we turned eighteen and went down to register for the draft, I was nervous about it — didn't like the idea of it. Tommy was like — it's never gonna happen. He said there's never gonna be a real war again — it's just going to be little scuffles. There's never gonna be a real war again . . .

HAL: You're supposed to trust your leader. I'm a businessman. I own a trophy shop. We have a good home and a good life and I thought I was raisin' my son to have the . . . evenhanded . . . views I have — had. I thought I was a good leader — good husband and dad. Think for yourself, son — think about things — if you think about things, you'll know what's right. You'll do what's right. How can this be right now? This ain't right, Jeff. This ain't at all right.

JEFF: Yes sir.

HAL: Pat Tillman was his hero.

JEFF: Yes — after he heard what he gave up. And then he died. But he wasn't even in the war — was he? He was in Afghanistan. Tommy was in the war.

HAL: I'm not sure what war this is.
(Pause.)
You heard me and your daddy go at a few times over the years.

JEFF: You sure can frustrate my old man, Hal. I love that.
(Hal gets up and opens the bottom drawer of his son's dresser. He pulls out a bottle of whiskey. He opens it and drinks then gives the bottle to Jeff, who takes a small swig.)
Between you and me, I'm surprised we never gave him a stroke.

HAL: Your daddy came to see me a couple of days after the funeral service . . . His opinions and his commitment were deeper than I'd ever seen 'em. We sat downstairs in the den and sipped scotch. I listened to him. Talking about how proud he was of Tommy. And I listened to him. I looked at your daddy, Jeff, and I had no clue about who in hell he was.
(Pause.)
A man I'd known for fifteen or sixteen some-odd years. Tellin' me how proud he was of my son. I never said much. Let your daddy do all the talking. Couple days after Tommy's funeral. I think I was still numb. Maybe I thought he could explain to me why I was wrong in thinkin' what I'd been thinkin'. Maybe If I listened to him I'd understand . . .

JEFF: Sure enough?

HAL: When he left he tried his best to give me a hug. He couldn't bring himself to do it — shoved his hand out so we could shake. Told me again how proud he was of us and of Tommy — for what he'd done for our country.

JEFF: He shakes my hand too . . .

HAL: I closed the door and walked upstairs. Came in here and sat on the bed. *(Pause.)* Numb. That was the night I knew I'd lost more than my son. My boy. Somethin' — gone . . .

JEFF: Maybe I should —

HAL: You're not goin' anywhere, Jeff.

(Hal hands the bottle back to Jeff. Jeff takes the bottle and sips. He sits in the chair at the desk.)

Follow the leader, remember? Schoolyard games to teach you discipline and character — leadership. Just because I didn't vote for the man, docsn't mean — didn't mean that I . . . I tried to relax myself into the fact that he was presidin' over us for his terms in office and he's a Goddamned liar, Jeff. Pretendin' to be a real Texan and he's from Goddamn Connecticut? That shouldda been everybody's first clue right there — he's just nothin' but a pretender — pretendin' he knows what the hell he's doin'. And I didn't stop my son from . . . I let him go — I let him make his own decision and —

JEFF: Maybe Libby could — maybe you should talk to —

HAL: Libby can't have this conversation with me. Libby doesn't know who I am anymore. Do you know who I am?

JEFF: You're my Best Man's dad. You're my friend too. The guy I thought sometimes, when I was a kid, that I could talk to about things when I couldn't talk to my own dad? You helped me a lot Hal.

HAL: But that's who I used to be, Jeff. The night your daddy stopped by for a visit — I shook his hand and said good night and realized I had nothing left — I don't know anything. I don't even believe in anything anymore.

JEFF: Yes you do, Hal — I know you . . .

HAL: I spend time in this room looking . . . I keep thinking I'll find it again — Understand. I know you loved him.

JEFF: He was my brother — if I was going to have a brother — he was my brother.

HAL: I stared at you all during his funeral. Your little gal holding your hand in both of hers. She was so lost. Libby's hand was so cold in mine. Your little gal . . . she didn't know what do with you — being such a mess. Had she ever seen you cry?

JEFF: I sure was a mess, wasn't I? No — she . . . no. I didn't know I could cry . . . like that.

HAL: Now see? If I knew who I was — I'd know what happened. I don't know what I'm gonna find in this room. But I'm waitin' to believe again. Even though I don't know what I'm gonna find. Is Tommy's ghost gonna come see me sittin' in here and kick my ass back into my life? Say "Daddy, what the hell're you doin'? Go make a trophy. Some kid just won a spellin' bee — some kid needs you." I can't do it. Jeff, I can't do it.

JEFF: Hal, I —

HAL: It's a brain tumor.

JEFF: I'm sorry . . .?

HAL: It's a car wreck.

JEFF: Hal?

HAL: If Tommy got a brain tumor and died of cancer — I'd know how — I'd know why. If he got in a car wreck . . . I'd feel cheated and robbed, but I'd understand. If I'd been born in the 1920s and lost my son in World War Two — I'd know — I'd understand — I think. But now. Not now. Because it just don't make a lick of sense to me and that makes me . . . I'm treadin' water, boy — new, weird water, and I'm sick and tired and I feel like I'm just about to drown. I can see the shore in the distance but it's too far away. Libby's waving her arms trying to get my attention, but I can't hear her calling me — because I'm too far out in the water.

JEFF: She needs you, Hal. Libby —

HAL: That's your little gal in the picture on the bulletin board?

JEFF: Yeah.

HAL: No more wars? just scuffles?

JEFF: Not a scuffle. Our first war.

HAL: Do you understand?

JEFF: I . . .

(Jeff loses it a little and takes the bottle.)

JEFF: I feel so fucked up about this right now . . . I . . . somebody took my . . . from six years old . . . I don't know what you feel inside, Hal, but I . . . A brain cancer — or a car wreck . . . I get it. I could — yeah. Yeah . . .

HAL: It is a car wreck — with a drunk driver — Bush is behind that wheel and he drove right into Iraq. You ever notice how when a drunk causes an wreck — most of the time they come off without a scratch or maybe a little beat up, but — it's everybody else who suffers or dies? But just about everybody seemed fine tellin' him he was OK to drive, didn't they?

(Silence.)

(Jeff takes a photo off the bulletin board.)

JEFF: One of the summers Tommy and I worked for you at your store.

HAL: You're . . .

JEFF: I 'member this T-shirt. I think this was the summer you — it is — we were takin' the recyclin' out to the alley and you caught us tryin' to smoke weed for the first time.

HAL: Let me see that.

(They trade the bottle for the photo.)

I'll be Goddamned.

JEFF: You never told my dad about that.

HAL: Hell no.

(Pause.)

Maybe you should think about askin' your daddy to be your Best Man.

JEFF: I made my decision. . . . I want you and Libby to come to the wedding, you know. Lisa really, really loved Tommy too and . . .

HAL: I wouldn't miss it for the world.

JEFF: I should . . .

HAL: Did he ever say anything to you about . . . anything? Did I ever — I feel so . . . I just flat out feel cheated. . . . years and years and years. And I . . .

JEFF: . . . I . . . *(Jeff shakes his head.)* I should . . . Mama's makin' supper. I just wanted to come by and see you. Say hi and let you know that . . . I was gonna honor Tommy this way. Let you know that his place beside me was . . . still his. Oh, and Mama wanted me to ask you and Libby if you wanted to come over — join us for supper. She said it'd been too long.

HAL: Did you ask Libby? What'd Libby say?

JEFF: She told me to ask you.

HAL: You tell your mama and daddy we said thank you but we got . . . thank her for us . . . ?

JEFF: I will. Um. I was thinking about going out to . . . to see Tommy's . . . grave . . . on Sunday before I . . . would you come on out there with me, maybe?

(Silence.)

OK. Well . . . I should . . .

HAL: I might want to take a drive on out there with you.

JEFF: That'd be . . . appreciate that.

HAL: Before you go: This Goddamn thing here . . .

(He picks up another remote.)

I can't for the life of me get this thing to work. I know what he watched. I was wondering . . . last time he was home — what he was listenin' to. I know there's one of them CD disks in there . . .

(Jeff sits on the bed next to Hal.)

JEFF: See this button. Press it . . . then press this one — whatever was playing . . . last time he was home . . .

(Jeff hugs Hal and heads for the door. He stops.)

So, I'll stop on by Sunday mornin' then?

(Hal nods. Jeff walks out. A moment. Hal flicks the button on the remote to Tommy's sound system. He presses play. Jamie Cullum's "All At Sea" begins to play:)

(Hal gets up and tacks the photo back on the bulletin board. He listens to the song, looking away from the photos.)

(Hal opens the desk drawer. He pokes around a moment and pulls out a bottle of cologne. He looks at the label as he closes the desk drawer. Hal contemplates the bottle of cologne.)

(Hal looks at the stereo and stops the song with the remote. He sits on the bed and looks around Tommy's room. Silence. Hal pulls the cap from the bottle of cologne and breathes it in. He sprays his son's fragrance into the air and breathes it in again. The lights fade away.)

END OF PLAY

Dead Boy

CRAIG WRIGHT

CHARACTERS

DEVON: sixteen, female
LARA: sixteen, female
BEN: sixteen, male

SETTING

The setting is a small room in an empty basement. There's a card table with four chairs around it. A Ouija board is on the table with its heart-shaped search device atop it.

TIME

The time is the present.

PERFORMANCE NOTES

Unless otherwise specified, all the dialogue should be essentially whispered, even if there are exclamation points.

Also, the last effect can be achieved with the help of an air slingshot.

• • •

Devon, Lara, and Ben are all seated at the table with their fingertips gently touching the plastic heart as it glides here and there across the Ouija board. The room is dark, lit only by four small candles near the four corners of the board.

ALL: *(Together, but not in precise unison, with long pauses in between.)* T. H. E.
BEN: "The."
LARA: Shut up.
BEN: Sorry.
ALL: *(After a long pause.)* Y.
LARA: See? You don't know when the word —
BEN: Shut up!
DEVON: Both you guys shut up. I swear.
ALL: *(With long pauses in between, as the heart moves.)* A. R. E.
BEN: *(Almost unconsciously.)* "Are."
LARA: Will you please tell your boyfriend to friggin' —
DEVON: Stop talking! Both of you!
BEN: Sorry. *(After a beat.)* God, you guys are bitches tonight.
LARA: Eat me.
BEN: You are.

LARA: YOU are.

BEN: You must be on your periods.

LARA: *(After a beat.)* Jesus McGillicuddy . . .

BEN: I'm serious.

LARA: What the hell does that mean anyway, "on" your period, who says that, Bonerface?

BEN: That's how you say it!

LARA: I don't say it that way.

BEN: That's how it's said!

LARA: *(To Devon.)* Do you say it that way, Devon? "On" your period?

DEVON: I don't know — no —

LARA: Like it's the friggin' horse you rode into Deadwood?

DEVON: You guys —

LARA: Hey, Tex, nice to see ya, I just rode into town "on" my period, I tied it to a post, and now I'm gonna go sit "on" my stool in the bar —

DEVON: You guys —

BEN: What?

DEVON: Are we gonna let the Dead Boy talk or not?

LARA: *(After a beat, referring to Ben.)* I don't care, he's the one moving it around anyway —

BEN: I am not.

LARA: Well, I'm not the one moving it, Gonad, I'm just going with what happens, so —

BEN: So am I.

LARA: So am I.

BEN: So am I.

LARA: Then she's the one.

DEVON: I'm not and, oh my God, you guys, check it out . . .

(The heart begins moving again, followed by fingertips.)

ALL: *(After a long pause, with pauses in between.)* H. E. *(After a very long pause.)* E. R. E.

BEN: *(After a very long, spooky pause.)* "They. Are. Here?"

LARA: *(Spooked.)* There were two *E*s.

DEVON: Yeah.

LARA: What's up with that?

DEVON: I don't know.

BEN: *(To Devon.)* What did you ask him?

DEVON: "Are you there," I think, right?

BEN: Yeah —

LARA: Yeah, you said, "Dead Boy, are you there?"

BEN: And he said, "They are here."

LARA: With two *E*'s.

BEN: Yeah.

DEVON: I'm scared.

LARA: So it's like, "They are hee—ee—re." *(After a pause.)* Like Old English or something. That's friggin' weird.

BEN: *(Thinking it through.)* "Are you there?" And he said, "They are here . . . "

LARA: What the hell does that mean?

BEN: I don't know.

LARA: "Are you there?" "They are here . . . " Devon?

DEVON: I don't know.

BEN: *(After a long spooky pause.)* Maybe he means us.

LARA: *(After a longer spookier pause.)* So then who's he talking to . . . ?

BEN: I don't know.

LARA: If he means us . . . ?

BEN: I don't know.

LARA: *(To Ben.)* There was only one, right?

BEN: In the house? Yeah.

LARA: There wasn't anybody else dead in the house when your grandma's family inherited it?

BEN: No. Not that I know of. Not that she said.

LARA: *(After a beat.)* "They are here."

BEN: *(After a beat.)* Maybe he's talking, like, in the spirit world, you know, so, he's not alone.

DEVON: Oh my God —

LARA: There are others.

DEVON: — that's so scary.

LARA: And whoever he's talking to, he's telling them we're here.

BEN: That means we're in the spirit world . . .

LARA: Yeah, or like, half in, half out.

(There's a long, spooky pause.)

DEVON: If you guys don't want to do this, we don't have to —

LARA: No, shut up —

DEVON: I'm just saying —

LARA: Ask him who "they" are. Ask him.

DEVON: I don't know if I want to.

LARA: This was your idea, Devon!

DEVON: I know, but —

LARA: I'll do it myself if I have to.

DEVON: *(To Ben.)* Do you wanna ask this time?

LARA: And don't talk when he answers, Talky McBigmouth.

BEN: Blow me.

LARA: Blow yourself.

DEVON: Just ask the question, you guys, I'm scared.

BEN: OK. *(After a long pause, to the Dead Boy.)* Dead Boy, who are they?
(They wait for a while. Nothing happens.)

LARA: He's gone for lunch or something —

DEVON: Shut up, he's waiting . . .

BEN: How do you know?

DEVON: I can feel it. *(After a beat.)* I don't wanna do this anymore.
(The heart starts moving.)

ALL: *(With pauses, some long, some short, in between.)* T. R. A. V. E. L. L. E. R. S.

LARA: *(After a long pause.)* Trah-vell-ers?

BEN: Travellers.

DEVON: With two *L*'s again, oh my God . . .

BEN: Like English.

DEVON: Yeah, like in "Into The West," I saw, they're like gypsies. "Travellers."
That's what they call themselves.

LARA: *(To Ben.)* Were they English people your Grandma's family inherited the
house from?

BEN: I don't know, she never said what they were. She just said they were cus-
tomers at the store. They left them the house in a will.

LARA: *(After a beat.)* Do you think he means them or us?

BEN: What do you mean?

LARA: When he said, "Travellers," did he mean them or us?

BEN: How do I know?

LARA: Ask him!

BEN: *(To the Dead Boy.)* Dead Boy, do you mean them or us? Are we the travellers?
*(The heart starts gliding immediately toward one of the bottom corners of the
board.)*

DEVON: Oh my God, you guys, where is it going?

BEN: In the corner.
(The heart goes to the corner and stays there.)

DEVON: Move it back.

BEN: I can't.

DEVON: Are you holding it there?

LARA: No.

DEVON: Ben, are you holding it there?

BEN: No!

DEVON: *(After a long pause.)* OK, then who's holding it?

BEN AND LARA: I don't know.

> *(After a beat, the heart starts shaking a little, rattling on the Ouija board. After a long moment, they all scream.)*

ALL: OW!

> *(And they all pull their hands away quickly. Devon stands and backs from the table.)*

DEVON: Oh my God, did you feel that, you guys?

LARA: Shit yeah!

DEVON: *(To Ben.)* Did you?

BEN: Yeah!

DEVON: What did that?

BEN: I don't know.

DEVON: You guys, what just did that?

LARA: I don't know!

DEVON: I don't know either!

LARA: It was cold, right?

BEN: Or hot.

DEVON: It was so cold it burned.

> *(They all sit there a moment, touching their fingertips.)*

DEVON: What could do that?

> *(After a beat, Ben reaches out and pokes the heart.)*

BEN: It feels normal.

LARA: Now.

> *(They stare at the heart a moment, genuinely frightened.)*

LARA: When do your parents get back?

BEN: I don't know, midnight, one, maybe.

LARA: They're gonna find us all, like, Blair Witched.

BEN: We should be videotaping this.

LARA: Geek squad.

BEN: Can you explain what just happened, Lara?

LARA: No!

BEN: So having it on videotape —

LARA: Would prove what, Gonad? That we all drank your gross gin and ton-
ics and lit a bunch of candles and freaked ourselves out?

DEVON: So you don't think it's real?

LARA: I don't know! How the hell should I know?

BEN: You felt it!

LARA: Yeah, I felt it, so what, feelings can be fake!

DEVON: I don't want to do it anymore.

LARA: That's fine with me.

BEN: I don't care.

DEVON: I don't want to. I'm sorry.

LARA: That's fine with me. It's all bullshit anyway.

(After a beat, with some trepidation, Devon taps the heart like it's a live, killer crab and pushes it off the board.)

LARA: *(After a beat, to Ben.)* Tell us again what the deal was.

BEN: Why?

LARA: Because I want to try and make sense of what he said, Gonad —

BEN: Stop calling me that!

LARA: Tell us what the deal was!

BEN: Even though it's all bullshit to you anyway.

LARA: Just tell the friggin' story. *(To Devon.)* By the way, the new minister at the church made me a mix CD.

DEVON: Of Christian music?

LARA: Some Christian and some real, it's so gross.

DEVON: That is gross.

LARA: It's, like, run your church or get a life, but either way, leave me the hell alone, you know? *(To Ben.)* Tell the deal.

BEN: OK. OK. *(After a beat, like a ghost story.)* My grandma's family was really poor, they had always lived in this, like, apartment above the grocery store in town that my great-grandfather worked at. And one day, this lawyer came into the store and told my great-grandfather he'd been left this house in a will, by an anonymous customer.

LARA: The house we're sitting in.

BEN: Yeah. So they moved in. It was all furnished and everything. The grandfather clock upstairs, the piano, that was all there when they got here. The other stuff, you know, it's all been replaced. But in my grandma's closet, they found this, like, false wall, behind the back of the closet, and when they pulled it, like, out, there was this little room.

DEVON: This room we're sitting in.

BEN: Yeah. But when they first opened it, there was, like, a cot, and a desk. And he was on the bed.

LARA: The Dead Boy.

BEN: Yeah. *(After a beat.)* He was chained to the bed.

LARA: This is such bullshit.

BEN: It is not.

LARA: So why was he chained to the bed?

BEN: Nobody knows.

LARA: Who was he?

BEN: Nobody knows. There was no record of a boy that age living in the house before, so no one knows. He just was . . . in there. Hidden. And everybody in the family was dead, so there was no one to ask. So. That was it.

LARA: And it was a customer who left him the —

BEN: Yeah. Just some guy who came into the store a lot, I guess. And liked it?

LARA: *(After a beat, thinking.)* A cot. A desk. And that was it.

BEN: There was, like, an old Bible. But it was in German.

LARA: So why does he spell like he's English?

BEN: I don't know.

DEVON: *(After a beat.)* Maybe it's not him.

LARA: Was he naked?

BEN: Yeah.

LARA: Gross.

BEN: And he was all, like, decayed. Grandma said he was, like, made of cobwebs, but with a face, like, made of old rotten handkerchiefs. He was all fragile.

LARA: That's so gross. Like he was a prisoner.

BEN: Or retarded or something.

LARA: That would explain the spelling.

DEVON: No it wouldn't.

BEN: English spelling is not retarded.

LARA: I was kidding! God, you two are the ones on your periods.

DEVON: *(After a beat, to Ben.)* You didn't move it, did you, when we were doing it? The heart?

BEN: No.

DEVON: *(To Lara.)* Did you?

LARA: No.

BEN: But, like you said, maybe it wasn't him. The one answering.

DEVON: But when I asked, I said, "Dead Boy, are you there?"

LARA: Yeah, that's what you said —

BEN: But —

DEVON: But WHAT?

BEN: I don't know. *(After a beat.)* I don't know.

(After a beat, Lara and Ben get up, spooked, and move away from the table. A moment passes.)

DEVON: You guys?

BEN: What?

DEVON: If you didn't move it, and you didn't move it, and I didn't move it, who moved it?

LARA: The Dead Boy.

DEVON: Or whoever it is answering the questions. Answering for the Dead Boy. In his place.

BEN: Yeah. His surrogate.

DEVON: In who?

BEN: *(After a beat.)* What do you mean?

DEVON: *(Scared, thinking it through.)* If the Dead Boy is moving the heart around on the board, and we're all touching the heart at the same time, then who is the Dead Boy in? When he answers the questions. Who is he in?

BEN: All of us. I guess.

LARA: Or just one, and the other two let it happen. Because I was just letting you two push it.

BEN: I wasn't pushing it.

DEVON: Neither was I.

LARA: Neither was I.

DEVON: So . . .

BEN: What? Devon. What?

DEVON: Is he in us now? Still?

(They all stand there a moment, trying to decide, trying to feel the Dead Boy's presence.)

LARA: Ask him.

DEVON: *(After a beat.)* OK.

(Devon goes to the table.)

LARA: No, just ask him!

DEVON: What do you mean?

LARA: Just ask him! If he's in us now, he can answer us without the stupid Ouija board thing. *(After a beat.)* Just ask him. Just ask him.

DEVON: *(After a beat, to the Dead Boy.)* Dead Boy . . . are you in us now?

(They all stand there, waiting for an answer.)

ALL: *(Quietly, almost in unison.)* Why?

DEVON: Oh my God, you guys . . .

LARA: *(To Ben.)* How did you do that?

BEN: Do what?

LARA: Get her to say "Why?"

BEN: I didn't!

LARA: Bullshit!

BEN: I didn't!

LARA: Bullshit, there's no way that happens, Ben!

BEN: I didn't get her to say anything!

LARA: Bullshit, if we were all trying to be, like, Power Rangers or make us shit ourselves for fun, we'd all say, "Yes," or something like, lame and typical, like that, but you guys started saying "Why" at the same time and then I just started saying it —

BEN: No, you guys started saying it —

DEVON: I did not!

BEN: We should stop.

DEVON: No!

BEN: Why not?

DEVON: Because, what if he's in us?

LARA: I don't want a Dead Boy in me.

BEN: He's not "in" us anymore anyway —

LARA: Gonad, she just asked him a question and we answered!

BEN: That was coincidence!

LARA: Ask another.

DEVON: No.

LARA: Ask another question!

DEVON: No!

(Suddenly — .)

ALL: *(In near unison.)* GET OUT! *(After a beat, similarly.)* GET OUT!
(They all look at each other, trying to figure out what's happening. They continue screaming in near-unison, terrified.)

ALL: GET OUT OF ME! GET OUT OF ME! STOP IT! GET OUT OF ME!
GET OUT! GET OUT OF ME! I DON'T WANT TO — GET OUT
OF ME! GET OUT! GET OUT!
(For a few moments, they all stand there, scared out of their minds, completely unaware of how that happened. Then:.)

BEN: Dev. Lara.

DEVON AND LARA: *(Not in unison.)* What?

BEN: Can I tell you guys something?

DEVON: What?

(A moment passes. An even deeper terror fills the trio.)

BEN: I made it all up. This is just, like, a storage room.

LARA: *(After a beat, still very tense.)* You dinkwad.

DEVON: *(After a long pause.)* So how did that happen?

BEN: Us all talking the same?

LARA: Yeah.

BEN: I don't know.

LARA: *(After a long pause, to Ben.)* You really made it up?

BEN: Yeah.

DEVON: All of it?

BEN: Yeah. *(After a beat.)* I think so. I mean, it came to me in my head. I don't know where I get my ideas, but . . . I made it up.

DEVON: *(After a long beat.)* So if I want to sit back down at the table now, it's just me, right?

BEN: Yeah.

DEVON: It's not the Dead Boy in me, saying he wants to sit down at the table and ask himself more questions?

BEN: No.

DEVON: It can't be.

BEN: Right.

DEVON: Because you made it all up.

BEN: Right.

DEVON: *(After a beat, slowly, methodically.)* And even if we go through the whole rest of our lives after this night, wondering if it's the Dead Boy inside us, moving us around, making us fall in love with who we fall in love with, picking our colleges, picking our jobs, making us feel feelings, basically, like, you know, like, living our lives through us . . . that can't be true, right? Because you just made it all up . . . right?

BEN: *(Somehow unsure.)* Right.

DEVON: *(Cautiously.)* OK. That's cool.

(They all quite fearfully, almost gingerly, sit back down at the table. Devon very cautiously puts the heart back in the center of the Ouija board. Checking in with each other in glances, they slowly put their fingertips on the heart. In near ceremonial unison, they all lean to the left and blow out three candles. One candle remains.)

ALL: *(In near unison, very slowly, very quietly.)* Dead Boy . . . are you there?

(They all look at each other, well aware they spoke in unison, spooked. They wait for an answer. Finally, it comes.)

ALL: No.

(A beat, and then, without anyone blowing, the fourth candle goes out, BOOM.)

END OF PLAY

PLAYS FOR
FOUR ACTORS

Vinny's Vision

JIM GORDON

The first production of *Vinny's Vision* was at the American Globe/Turnip Theatre Company in New York, with the following cast: Mike: Mike Boland; Vinny: Jim Gordon; Tony: Frank Mollica; Jimmy: Tom Rushen. Director: Lester Colodny.

Winner of the Alan Minieri Award for playwriting excellence, presented by the Turnip Theatre Co.

CHARACTERS
    MIKE: thirties
    VINNY: thirty-five to forty
    TONY: thirties
    JIMMY: thirties

SETTING
    The play takes place in the back room of a neighborhood tavern. The only
    furniture in the room is a card table, four chairs. The television is assumed.

SYNOPSIS:
    A death in the family has depressed and angered Mike. Three friends
    decide their sympathetic approach has not helped their buddy overcome
    his grief. Something unconventional must be tried. A tearjerker for tough
    guys.

•   •   •

*At Rise: We're in the back room of a tavern. Tony, Mike, Jimmy, and Vinny
are watching the finish of a close horse race.*

TV ANNOUNCER: ". . . and it's Maureen's Momma by a nose, Kitty Kat second,
    and Milo's Prince a close third . . ."
    (Jimmy turns off the TV.)
TONY: I told you didn't I . . . didn't I tell you —
MIKE: Bullshit!
TONY: C'mon, I told you, sure I did.
JIMMY: He did, he said that, Maureen's Momma, I heard him.
MIKE: Then why didn't he bet her? Why didn't you bet her, smart ass?
TONY: Who said I didn't?
JIMMY: Did ya, Tony, you bet Momma?
TONY: Maybe, maybe not.
MIKE: You're full a shit, you know that, your full a shit!
JIMMY: Who'd you have Vinny?
VINNY: Momma.
JIMMY: Hey, no shit?
MIKE: Let's play cards.
TONY: You did, you bet Momma? No shit!
JIMMY: Whose deal?
MIKE: They're already dealt, stupid.

JIMMY: Don't take it out on me.

MIKE: I bet a buck.

VINNY: Five bucks.

JIMMY: Not me. I'm out.

MIKE: FIVE BUCKS?

JIMMY: He bet Momma, he can afford it.

TONY: Not with these. I'm gone.

MIKE: *(Mike, unhappy, tosses five dollars in the pot.)* Give me one.

VINNY: Same here.

MIKE: A buck.

VINNY: Cost you five more.

> *(He throws five dollars in the pot. Mike, follows.)*

MIKE: What?

VINNY: Full house.

MIKE: *(Angry, he flings his cards on the table.)* Fuck you!

JIMMY: *(Laughing.)* Sore loser, sore loser . . .

TONY: Hey Vinny, that's four winners in a row.

JIMMY: Don't forget Momma. It's five counting Momma. I'll bet he's taking lessons. You taking lessons, Vinny?

VINNY: No, no lessons.

MIKE: Fucking lucky, that's all.

JIMMY: What gives, Vinny?

VINNY: I had a vision.

> *(Everyone stares at Vinny as he deals the cards.)*

MIKE: What the hell are you talking about, "You had a vision?"

VINNY: I had a vision.

TONY: Like a dream, you mean?

VINNY: No, like a vision. Ever since I've been lucky.

TONY: You mean like that Lourdes thing, huh? That kind of vision?

JIMMY: Yeah, like those kids saw, you know, in that movie, what was it, *Song of the South.*

MIKE: You're a dumb shit, you know that? It was *The Song of Benadette.* What a dumb shit!

VINNY: *(To Jimmy.)* Your bet.

MIKE: Wait a second. I want to know about this vision thing.

TONY: What did you see? This vision, who was it?

MIKE: I'm not playing cards with some guy who's fucking seeing things.

TONY: Was it people you saw, you know, like . . . people?

VINNY: There were people, yeah.

JIMMY: Anyone we know?

MIKE: Will you shut up!

JIMMY: I meant people like us.

MIKE: There's no one like you. *Song of the South.* Jesus, what a dumb bastard.

JIMMY: What horse did you bet, smart ass?" Calling me dumb.

VINNY: We going to play or what?

MIKE: I'm not playing cards with some guy who's seeing things; no way I'm playing cards with a psychotic.

JIMMY: It's psychic stupid, not psychotic.

TONY: Where were you when you saw this thing? You in a church or what?

MIKE: Vinny in a church? Are you shitting me?

VINNY: The Motor Vehicle Bureau.

(Silence.)

MIKE: The Motor Vehicle Bureau?

VINNY: Yeah.

MIKE: *(He gets up to leave.)* That's it; I'm out of here . . .

TONY: No, let's hear this.

VINNY: I'm renewing my license and they give you a number. So they give me this number, and I'm sitting there, you know, waiting for them to call my number. It was sixty-four, I think . . . maybe it was sixty-five. Yeah, it was sixty-five. Well, anyway . . . no, no wait a second, it was sixty-four, I'm sure it was sixty-four, because the guy next to me had sixty-three —

MIKE: Will you stop with the fucking numbers . . .

TONY: C'mon, let him finish.

MIKE: Jesus . . .

JIMMY: So, what happened?

VINNY: I hear someone say, "It's your turn, Vinny."

JIMMY: Someone called your number?

TONY: They don't call your number.

VINNY: No, that's the thing, no one calls your number, it comes up on this thing. Anyway, I hear, "It's your turn, Vinny," so not thinking, I gets up to walk to the window, but I see the number on the thing that shows the numbers says thirty-six, not sixty-four, and like I said, I had sixty-four. So I says, what's up, you know?

MIKE: You going to finish this, or what?

TONY: Ignore him.

VINNY: Now I'm standing there like a jerk, looking around, holding this number 64, and I says to myself, hey Vinny, you must be hearing things. Then this voice says, "No Vinny, you're not hearing things — over here." I turns around, and there's this guy at the window, old guy with gray hair, and there's no line. I mean no line at the Motor Vehicle Bureau, there's a fucking miracle right there.

MIKE: He's never going to finish this. I swear he's never going to finish this.

TONY: C'mon, what happened?

VINNY: Now I'm at the window, and this old guy with the gray hair takes my papers and says, "everything's OK." So I says, it's good everything's OK cause I need a license, you know, and he says, "No, not your license . . . Christina . . . Christina's OK."

TONY: He said Christina's OK?

JIMMY: No shit, he said that? Christina's OK. He said that?

VINNY: Christina is fine, that's what he said. Well, the only Christina I know is my mother, and she's dead! Then he says . . . "She said to say hello."

TONY: Ah, c'mon, Vinny.

JIMMY: She said to say hello, no shit.

VINNY: I swear that's what this guy says, "She said to say hello."

JIMMY: Jesus. Sounds like that program, ya know, *The Sunset Zone.*

MIKE: *Twilight Zone,* asshole!

VINNY: So I'm looking around for the camera. I figure it's one of those practical joke things, you know, but who the hell would do a rotten thing like that, I mean, who'd do that?

MIKE: Now they'll build a grotto in a fucking motor vehicle bureau.

TONY: What else he say, this guy?

VINNY: I don't know . . .

JIMMY: He said, "I don't know?"

VINNY: No, I mean I don't know if I should say . . . you know . . . what he said.

TONY: What's the matter?

VINNY: Well, it's just —

MIKE: What bullshit!

VINNY: I don't blame you for thinking that, Mike, I really don't, but it ain't bullshit. I'm telling you it happened — just like that it happened.

MIKE: I'll break your Goddamn neck if you don't finish this.

TONY: Go ahead, Vinny. What he say?

VINNY: Well he says . . .

JIMMY: Yeah? Go on, go ahead.

VINNY: He says . . . "Tell Mike not to worry; Jeanie's OK."

MIKE: *(Beat.)* What did you say?

VINNY: That's what the guy said, "Tell Mike not to worry, Jeanie's OK."

MIKE: *(Mike lunges for Vinny.)* You lying bastard, you son of a bitch . . .
    (Jimmy and Tony get between Mike and Vinny.)

TONY: Stop it Mike. For crissakes, he wouldn't make that up.

JIMMY: C'mon Mike, take it easy . . .

MIKE: You lying bastard.

VINNY: I'm not lying. I wouldn't lie about that.

TONY: He wouldn't lie about that, Mike.

VINNY: I'm telling you, it's what I heard.

JIMMY: *(Mike sits — A long pause.)* Gee, isn't that something?

VINNY: *(After a moment.)* I'm sorry Mike, I'm sorry I upset you. I didn't mean to upset you.

TONY: He say anything else, this guy?

VINNY: He hands me my license and walks away. Well, I'm standing there, you know, waiting for this guy to come back, but he doesn't come back. So I ask the guy in the next window when his neighbor's coming back, and he looks at me like I'm crazy. What the hell are you talking about, he says, that window ain't been used for six months.

JIMMY: Six months? No shit!

TONY: *(Pause.)* You OK Mike?

VINNY: I'm sorry, Mike, but that's what he said, "Tell Mike not to worry; Jeanie's OK."

JIMMY: He really said that, uh?

VINNY: I know, it's crazy! I'm sorry, Mike, I . . . I thought you'd want to know. I'm sorry I upset you.

(Mike begins to cry. The other men appear uncomfortable. They've never seen Mike cry.)

TONY: *(Pause. To Mike.)* You OK?

JIMMY: You all right, Mike?

MIKE: *(Beat.)* Yeah . . .

TONY: You sure?

MIKE: Yeah . . . I'm all right.

VINNY: I'm sorry I upset you, Mike. I didn't mean to.

MIKE: Jeanie's OK . . . he said that?

VINNY: Yeah Mike, he did . . . and not to worry.

MIKE: Yeah.

(Pause.)

I gotta go.

JIMMY, VINNY, TONY: Sure. Yeah. Hey, no problem.

TONY: We'll catch you tomorrow, OK?

MIKE: Yeah . . . tomorrow.

VINNY: Take care, Mike.

JIMMY: Yeah Mike, you take care, huh?

MIKE: You too . . . you take care.

(Mike exits. After a moment.)

VINNY: He all right?

TONY: Yeah, he's OK.

VINNY: *(They take their seats. A pause.)* Well . . . what do you think? You think it helped?

TONY: I think so.

(To Jimmy.)

What do you think?

JIMMY: Yeah . . . I think so . . . yeah.

TONY: You did good, Vinny.

JIMMY: C'mon! We all did good.

TONY: Yeah. Yeah I think so.

JIMMY: *(Beat.)* Hey Vinny?

VINNY: What?

JIMMY: *(Beat.)* That guy at the Motor Vehicle Bureau . . . he really say that?

(Vinny and Tony stare at Jimmy in disbelief, as the lights fade to black.)

END OF PLAY

Betting the Karmic House

BILL JOHNSON

CHARACTERS

    FRED: middle-aged, dressed like he's been out in the snow
    MURIEL: middle-aged, silk clothes loose and flowing
    BLACKJACK DEALER: a man in a black suit and string tie
    ANNOUNCER: an unseen, upbeat voice

SETTING

    A blackjack table, chairs

• • •

At Open: Muriel plays blackjack with a Dealer.

DEALER: Blackjack.
    (Slides some chips to her already large pile.)
    One million dollars.
MURIEL: Let it ride.
    (The Dealer deals another hand.)
DEALER: Blackjack.
    (Slides more chips across the table.)
    Five million dollars.
MURIEL: Let it ride.
    (Fred approaches and watches as the Dealer deals another hand.)
DEALER: Blackjack.
    (Slides over more chips.)
    Twenty-five million dollars.
    (Fred sits beside Muriel.)
MURIEL: *(To Dealer.)* Let it ride.
    (To Fred.)
    You still trying to help Scott make it back from the Antarctic?
FRED: Something to do. Winning?
    (Dealer sets out another hand.)
DEALER: *(Sliding more chips to her.)* Blackjack. One hundred million dollars.
MURIEL: So so.
FRED: I saw Elvis.
MURIEL: No. Where?
    (To Dealer.)
    Let it ride.
FRED: Doing a lounge act.

MURIEL: Oh, Fred, there are more Elvises here than a karaoke bar in Memphis.

FRED: So where is he? Your room?

(Dealer sets out another hand.)

MURIEL: Well, if you must know, yes.

DEALER: Blackjack. One billion dollars.

(He slides more chips toward Muriel.)

FRED: What are you going to do with a billion dollars?

MURIEL: Well, in this place, a billion dollars, a banana, three scoops of ice cream, and some chocolate syrup will get me a banana split.

FRED: I won five billion last week.

MURIEL: What'd you do with it?

FRED: Bought Marilyn Monroe a cup of tea before she went to her acting class. She's still determined to get it right.

FRED: How much longer before we go back?

ANNOUNCER: *(Voice-over.)* Welcome to Astral Las Vegas, where every bet is a winner, and our cocktail angels are eager to shake their tail feathers to serve you. Don't be shy, sign up to be a heavenly lounge backup singer and get up and sing with Sinatra.

MURIEL: Not soon enough. I'm bored to death.

FRED: I'd even agree to go back as a gay Republican environmentalist schoolteacher in Texas if that meant I could blow this astral pop stand.

DEALER: If you're looking for excitement, there is another game you could play.

MURIEL: We're all ears.

DEALER: We're allowing people to place bets with their karma tonight.

MURIEL: You mean if I win, I could have a better life to go back to?

DEALER: Yes.

FRED: But if I lose . . .

DEALER: Then you lose some of your good karma.

MURIEL: How does that apply to relationships? I mean, if he loses, and we're together . . .

DEALER: If he wins, you win. If he loses, and you're together, you both lose.

FRED: What about body types? Can I bet on that?

DEALER: Yes, sir.

MURIEL: Wait a minute, you mean he can win a bet that I'd have a more attractive body in our next life?

DEALER: No, just his own.

FRED: Good enough for me. When can we start?

MURIEL: But what if he loses? Does he go from a young Marlon Brando to the . . . older version?

DEALER: It depends on the nature of the bet.

FRED: I'm just going to ask this straight out, could I win a better wife?

MURIEL: Better? You're lucky to have me.

FRED: It's just a question. Aren't we supposed to be thinking about how we could do better in our next lifetime?

MURIEL: That means improving yourself, not improving me.

FRED: Fine. But if I lose my karmic shirt and pants, you're still going to be left holding my . . .

MURIEL: Fred, I forbid this.

(To Dealer.)

Can't I?

DEALER: You can only bet your own karma, ma'am.

FRED: Ha ha ha. This is great.

MURIEL: Are you serious?

FRED: I won five billion dollars last week? I'm on a roll, baby.

MURIEL: The only roll you've been on your last three lifetimes is day-old bear claws. I'm sick of the smell.

FRED: That's my first bet, then.

MURIEL: What?

FRED: *(To Dealer.)* I want to bet my pastry karma.

DEALER: Yes, sir.

(Dealer deals.)

MURIEL: What in the hell is pastry karma?

DEALER: Nineteen.

FRED: *(To Muriel.)* What should I do?

MURIEL: Have you ever gotten a number lower than twenty before tonight?

(The Dealer deals his cards.)

DEALER: Twelve.

FRED: I don't think so.

DEALER: *(Deals another card.)* Eighteen.

MURIEL: I don't like this.

DEALER: *(Deals himself a four.)* Twenty-two. We have a winner.

FRED: Yes, yes, yes!

MURIEL: What yes, yes, yes? What about your cholesterol? That truck tire around your waist in your next life will be the size of New Jersey.

FRED: *(To Dealer.)* Can I bet that scientists will come up with a low-fat, low-cholesterol pastry?

MURIEL: That tastes good.

FRED: Hey, now you're getting into it.

(To Dealer.)

That tastes good.

DEALER: The bet is on the table.

(The Dealer deals. The Dealer has an ace of spades face up. Fred gets sixteen.)

DEALER: Sixteen.

MURIEL: I don't like this.

FRED: Let me think, let me think.

(Fred stares at cards. Smiles at Dealer.)

FRED: Could I get a lifeline here?

DEALER: Sorry, sir, we don't offer reality programming. I'm told in that other place, it's available twenty-four hours a day.

MURIEL: That would be hell.

DEALER: Oh, no, ma'am, it's by request.

(To Fred.)

What would you like to do, sir?

(Fred rocks on his stool.)

FRED: I'm gonna . . . I'm gonna . . .

MURIEL: Stay, stay, stay.

FRED: Hit me!

(Fred gets another card, a four.)

DEALER: Twenty.

MURIEL: Thank God.

FRED: But he could have a face card to go with that ace?

MURIEL: You can't bet on getting an ace.

FRED: Yes, I can. This is heaven.

DEALER: Indeed it is, sir.

FRED: Hit me.

(Fred gets a spade king.)

DEALER: Spade king. Dealer wins.

MURIEL: Oh my God, in my next life I'm going to be married to the Fat Bastard.

FRED: God dammit, you threw off my concentration, Muriel. I needed to concentrate.

(Muriel grabs Fred by the arm.)

MURIEL: Fred, it's time to go.

FRED: No, it was one bad hand. I want to bet that in my next life, I get to live in a mansion.

MURIEL: Be careful! You want to be a servant?

FRED: *(To Dealer.)* Right, I want to own the mansion, mortgage paid off.

(To Muriel.)

You want servants? A guesthouse?

MURIEL: A heated indoor pool with a sauna . . .

FRED: *(To dealer.)* With a heated indoor pool and sauna.

MURIEL: I'm still against this, but if you're going to do it . . .

FRED: What? Name it, baby.

MURIEL: Woodpeckers.

FRED: Woodpeckers?

MURIEL: I like the sound.

FRED: That's the bet. Deal.

> *(The Dealer deals.)*

DEALER: Blackjack.

> *(Fred and Muriel jump into each others arms.)*

MURIEL: You were right to keep betting, but it's time to stop now.

FRED: Stop? But I'm on a roll.

MURIEL: But this is our life.

DEALER: We have time for one more bet.

> *(Muriel pushes Fred off the betting stool and sits in his place.)*

MURIEL: I want to bet that in spite of his bets, we'll have just the life we were
  supposed to have.

FRED: But, Muriel, we could be somebody.

MURIEL: Aren't I enough for you?

FRED: I may be enough for you, but I'm not enough for myself. Just let me do
  one more bet.

MURIEL: Is it really that important to you?

FRED: It is.

> *(Muriel considers, then lets Fred sit.)*

FRED: I want to own a football team that wins the Super Bowl.

DEALER: That would require all your good karma.

MURIEL: Fred, don't.

FRED: I have to.

> *(Dealer deals.)*

DEALER: King and Queen; twenty.

FRED: Please, please, please . . .

MURIEL: I can't watch.

> *(She tries not to look, but does. Dealer plays his cards; blackjack.)*

DEALER: Dealer wins.

FRED: Shit. Shit. Shit. What will I be now?

MURIEL: What will WE be? Homeless street people?

FRED: I'm so sorry, I . . .

ANNOUNCER: *(Voice-over.)* Welcome to Astral Las Vegas, where every bet wins.

Just a reminder, you can only bet with astral dollars; betting earthly karma is not allowed.

FRED: *(To Dealer.)* You lied to me . . . to us.

(Dealer closes the game.)

DEALER: Yes, sir.

MURIEL: Why?

DEALER: You were bored. Now you're not.

(He leaves.)

FRED: What a relief.

MURIEL: I would have asked for a new car every ten years, and a neighborhood with good schools for our children.

(She turns to go, stops by the edge of the stage.)

FRED: We can have that, the two of us, we're a team.

MURIEL: Now that I know what you really want, I'll have to think about our sharing another life together.

FRED: How about double or nothing?

MURIEL: You just did, Fred. And you lost.

(She exits.)

FRED: *(After Muriel.)* I just wanted to be somebody.

(Lights fade.)

FRED: Double or nothing. Anybody?

END OF PLAY

Infant Morality

CRAIG POSPISIL

Infant Morality was first produced by the Workshop at the
Neighborhood Playhouse (Harold Baldridge, Artistic Director.)
in New York in November 1999. It was directed by James
Alexander Bond, and the cast was as follows: Trish: Darcie
Siciliano; Stephanie Hackett: Leah Herman; Philip Hackett:
Troy Myers; Pamela Warden: Mari Gorman. The play was sub-
sequently staged by Playwrights Actors Contemporary Theater
(Jane Petrov, Artistic Director.) on May 19, 2005. It was direct-
ed by Greg Skura, and the cast was as follows: Trish: Ashlie
Atkinson; Stephanie Hackett: Nicole Taylor; Philip Hackett:
Rowland Hunt; Pamela Warden: Jill Van Note.

CHARACTERS

TRISH: twenties to thirties, a nurse

STEPHANIE: thirties, affluent, and feels entitled

PHILIP HACKETT: thirties, Stephanie's husband, feels the same

PAMELA WARDEN: thirties/forties/fifties, efficient and direct

SETTING

The front desk in the admitting room of a hospital

TIME

The present

• • •

A hospital admitting room. A nurse, Trish, is behind the main counter doing paperwork. Stephanie enters. She carries a large shopping bag from an expensive store.

STEPHANIE: Excuse me.

TRISH: Yes, can I help you?

STEPHANIE: Yes, I have something I'd like to return.

TRISH: To return?

STEPHANIE: I got it here a few weeks ago, and . . . well, it's not me. It's just not comfortable.

(Stephanie puts the shopping bag on the counter. Trish looks at it, confused.)

TRISH: Ma'am, . . . this is a hospital.

STEPHANIE: Yes, I know. My name is Stephanie Hackett. I was in here about three weeks ago. That's when I got it.

TRISH: *(She looks in the bag.)* Ma'am, it's just that . . . oh my God! This is a baby!

STEPHANIE: I'm sorry to be a bother, but I'm an investment banker, you see, and, well, I thought I could bring it to the office. You know, like in one of those cute little papoose things. But it just sat and whimpered in the corner while I was working, and I couldn't concentrate. And my husband travels a lot for business . . . so, I'd like to return it and get a refund.

TRISH: What are you talking about?

STEPHANIE: Is your hearing all right? I want to return this baby.

TRISH: You can't do that!

STEPHANIE: What do you mean?

TRISH: It's your baby!

STEPHANIE: Yes, and I don't want it anymore. I just finished explaining the situation.

TRISH: But we can't take them back!

STEPHANIE: Nonsense. Everyone has a return policy. So don't . . . Oh! You probably need the receipt! Why didn't you just say so? *(She digs in her purse.)* Of course you need that. Otherwise I could've gotten this anywhere. Sorry. Here it is.

TRISH: No, I don't need a receipt. You didn't pay for the baby.

STEPHANIE: We certainly did. And it was very expensive too. Now, my husband is double-parked outside, so I don't have a lot of time here.

TRISH: Is this some kind of joke?

STEPHANIE: Are you new on the job? It's a baby.

(Slight pause.)

Are you saying you're not going to take it back?

TRISH: Finally!!

STEPHANIE: Well, this is ridiculous. I mean, if I'd known that, we'd've gone to another hospital.

(Slight pause.)

I want to speak to the manager.

TRISH: What?

STEPHANIE: You get the manager down here right now. I'm not going to stand for this. I want a full refund. And not credit. Cash.

(The sounds of a baby crying emanate from the bag. Stephanie hits the bag.)

STEPHANIE: Oh, shut up! See?! It was like this all the time!

TRISH: *(Slight pause.)* I'll call the hospital administrator. You can take this up with her.

STEPHANIE: Thank you.

(Trish picks up a telephone and dials. As she speaks on the phone. Philip enters. He frowns and crosses to Stephanie.)

PHILIP: Honey, what's going on? The appointment's for 2:30.

STEPHANIE: She says they don't accept returns or give refunds.

PHILIP: What? You showed her the receipt, right?

STEPHANIE: Of course, I did.

(Trish hangs up and turns to the couple.)

TRISH: The hospital administrator will be right down.

PHILIP: What kind of an operation are you running here?!

TRISH: Sir, please lower your voice. This is a hospital.

PHILIP: And a pretty damn poor one too!

TRISH: Sir, if you don't quiet down, I'll have to call security.

PHILIP: You go ahead and call. If they touch me, I'll sue this place so fast it'll make your head spin.

(The man pulls out a cellular phone, which he brandishes like a club.)

TRISH: My head is already spinning.

STEPHANIE: Can you believe the way she talks?

(To the nurse.)

Are you familiar with the phrase, "The customer is always right"?

TRISH: Are you familiar with the phrase, "Crazy as a loon"?

(The baby cries again. Stephanie throws her hands up. Philip comforts her.)

STEPHANIE: Again with that noise.

PHILIP: Don't worry. We'll get this taken care of.

STEPHANIE: I told you a baby would be nothing but trouble.

PHILIP: I know. I'm sorry, Steph. I thought it would be different. This is all my fault.

STEPHANIE: Oh, no. It's not you.

(Indicating Trish.)

It's her I blame. I just want to put this behind us so we can go on with our lives.

PHILIP: *(To Trish.)* Look, the agreement my lawyer can't find a loophole in hasn't been written. So, why don't you just take it back and we'll forget your rudeness.

TRISH: In a second, I'm going to do something to you with that cell phone that'll make your wife's labor pains seem like stubbing a toe.

PHILIP: OK . . . OK. Let's start over. I may have overreacted. I'm sorry I raised my voice. *(He pauses and leans forward.)* Now, . . . why don't you just tell me what it'll take to make this problem go away.

(Slight pause.)

How does two hundred dollars sound?

TRISH: You must be joking.

PHILIP: OK. You play hardball. I can respect that. All right, five hundred.

TRISH: Oh, that's it! I'm gonna —

(The hospital administrator, Warden, enters.)

WARDEN: What's the problem, Trish?

TRISH: I am so glad you're here.

PHILIP: Your name is?

WARDEN: I'm Pamela Warden, the hospital administrator. And you are . . . ?

PHILIP: Philip Hackett, and this is my wife, Stephanie.

STEPHANIE: We came to return something, and this woman has been exceedingly rude to us.

WARDEN: Wait . . . "return"? Return what?

TRISH: Their baby! They got it here . . . I mean, they had it here three weeks ago. Now they don't want it and they want their money back!

WARDEN: A refund?

TRISH: Yes. And when I told them we wouldn't take it, he tried to bribe me.

STEPHANIE: That's a lie! She tried to extort money from us.

PHILIP: I don't understand why you people are having such a hard time with this.

WARDEN: You can't "return" a child.

STEPHANIE: Well, that simply wasn't made clear to us. And that being the case, I feel the hospital should do the right thing.

WARDEN: I think this is a matter for the police.

PHILIP: That's it! I'm going to sue this hospital for every penny it has. We paid good money, and when we were dissatisfied you had an obligation to make proper restitution, but instead we've been insulted and made to waste our time.

STEPHANIE: And our time is very important.

WARDEN: You don't intimidate me. I can have child welfare here in five minutes. And then I think we'll be seeing you on the six o'clock news!

(The couple heads down into one corner of the stage to speak with their lawyer.)

PHILIP: *(He dials his phone.)* Yes, Ted Pendleton please. Philip Hackett calling. *(The couple huddles around the cellular phone, and the rest of the conversation cannot be heard. Warden and Trish remain by the counter as Warden flips through a phone book. The telephone on the counter rings, and Trish answers it.)*

TRISH: Front desk? Yes, she's right here.

(She hands Warden the phone.)

It's your secretary.

WARDEN: Yes, Jen?

(Slight pause.)

What? He didn't! Do the parents know?

(Slight pause.)

All right, don't say anything. I'll be right up.

TRISH: What's happening?

WARDEN: Dr. Henderson was delivering a baby, and there were . . . complications. I've asked the board not to let him . . . well, anyway it's dead. The baby's parents, the Kendalls don't know yet. Henderson snuck the body out of the delivery room. I have to tell them.

(Slight pause.)

You'll have to deal with these two.

TRISH: Oh, of course. I'll finish calling —

(Trish picks up the phone to dial, but Warden breaks the connection.)

WARDEN: Wait a second.

(On the other side of the stage, Philip switches off his phone.)

PHILIP: He says we don't have a case.

STEPHANIE: What do you mean?

PHILIP: That's what he says. Unless we can prove the baby is defective, and that it's the hospital's fault.

STEPHANIE: Well, it cries and defecates all the time.

PHILIP: He said he thought that was normal.

STEPHANIE: What are we going to do now?

PHILIP: We could try and bluff them.

STEPHANIE: Bluff them? That's the best you've got?

PHILIP: Can you think of anything better?

STEPHANIE: Maybe we could give it to someone. Like as a housewarming gift. Or for a birthday.

(The couple confers quietly as Trish and Warden resume talking.)

WARDEN: It's the perfect solution.

TRISH: What?!

WARDEN: Think of it as a total organ transplant. But without the surgery.

TRISH: But the Kendall's should know their baby died.

WARDEN: Our job is to alleviate pain and suffering. Are you asking me to inflict the worst kind of emotional pain on them? Have some decency.

TRISH: But this is no better than what the Hacketts are trying to do.

WARDEN: Trish, I have to weigh all the pros and cons here. Right now we're facing two potential lawsuits. I can stop both of them before they start.

TRISH: Money? That's what you're worried about?

WARDEN: Do you know what this could cost the hospital? Hm? Court costs, skyrocketing insurance premiums. Millions. And that means doctors taking pay cuts . . . nurses fired. Do you want to be responsible for that? Try to look at the big picture.

TRISH: It's not right.

WARDEN: Right, wrong . . . We're dealing with larger issues here. Shrinking profit margins, for one.

TRISH: But the Kendall's lost their child. This baby's parents are right here.

WARDEN: Do you know who the Kendall's are? They're very wealthy. This child could have the best nannies and be sent to the best boarding schools. It might even have a pony. But you want to take that all away.

TRISH: Well, no, . . . I . . . the Hacketts are terrible, yes, but the child should be —

WARDEN: Put into foster care? Shuffled from one home to another, grasping for some sense of stability for the rest of it's life?

TRISH: No, it should be put up for adoption. It should be placed in a loving home, with a good couple who really want a child and will love her and always take care of her.

WARDEN: Trish, . . . no one has that.

(The Hacketts stride over to the counter. Warden, smiling, turns to face them.)

PHILIP: Our lawyer advised us to try and talk things over with you more, and see if we can't avoid a court battle.

WARDEN: Oh, absolutely. In fact, I've been reviewing some of our bylaws and I've found there is a procedure for the return of infants who . . . haven't met the expected standards of the parents.

TRISH: You can't do this.

WARDEN: Trish, you've caused enough trouble. In fact, I think you should apologize to the Hacketts.

TRISH: Apologize!!?

STEPHANIE: I don't know what terrible things have happened to you, but you don't help anything by going around with a chip on your shoulder. It's very unattractive.

PHILIP: Can we get this done?

WARDEN: Absolutely. I'll have you out of here in ten minutes.

STEPHANIE: You've been such a help.

WARDEN: Oh, please, I'm just doing my job.

(She indicates the hallway and the Hacketts exit.)

WARDEN: Be in my office tomorrow at nine. It's time for your job performance review.

(Slight pause.)

I wonder if the morgue might not be a better assignment for you.

(Warden exits after the Hacketts. Trish is left alone. She turns and notices they have left the shopping bag with the baby. She rushes over and peeks inside.)

TRISH: Hello there. They forgot all about you. Are you all right?

(She pulls a bundle out of the bag and cradles it.)

TRISH: Oh, aren't you adorable. I'm sorry. I tried, but . . . . Well, don't worry. I guess you'll be getting a new home. And a pony.

(Slight pause.)

What's your name? Did they give you one? I'm Trish.

(She smiles at the baby, and then looks down the hallway. She looks back at the baby.)

TRISH: But you can call me Mommy.
(Trish hurries out of the hospital carrying the baby.)
(Blackout.)

END OF PLAY

How To Speak Man

A short lesson for the stage

SHARYN ROTHSTEIN

CHARACTERS

Three work buddies in their mid-twenties to late forties, in typical office attire:

CHARLIE KRONE

TOM FINEBERG

ALAN SPALDING

And their boss, a jovial man's man with a rhetorical sense of humor:

RANDY QUIGLEY

SETTING

The modern office

•   •   •

An office. Monday morning. Charlie Krone, Tom Fineberg, and Alan Spalding have just arrived at their respective desks.

CHARLIE: So I wake up and I'm all tied down. I mean, head to foot, tied down to the bed. I'm thinking, OK, either last night was really good or it was really bad.

(A dramatic pause.)

And then my mother walks in.

TOM: Bullshit.

SPALDING: Tom, did you get Quigley the Landon materials before you left Friday?

TOM: Yeah, of course.

CHARLIE: You're not even going to let me finish?

TOM: No, I'm not even going to let you finish. Spalding, are you listening to this?

SPALDING: What?

TOM: Krone's bullshit-my-mom's-the-city's-most-famous-dominatrix story.

CHARLIE: Spalding already knows. Who do you think her biggest client is?

(Charlie and Tom laugh and wait for Spalding's rebuttal. There is none. Spalding continues organizing his desk. Beat.)

SPALDING: Does anybody have a stapler remover?

CHARLIE: What's wrong with you?

SPALDING: Nothing. Why?

TOM: You just seem . . . Weird.

SPALDING: Do I? Huh. Maybe you're right. I do feel a bit off. Like I'm not quite myself today or something. *(Beat.)* I think I'm just very fragile today.

(Charlie and Tom freeze. They stare at Spalding. Spalding, not noticing their stares, takes a sip of his coffee.)

TOM: "Fragile"?

SPALDING: Like if you touched me the wrong way I could just break into a million pieces. Do you guys ever feel that way?

(Beat. Charlie and Tom look at each other.)

TOM/CHARLIE: *(Protesting too much . . .)* No. No. Never. I don't even know what you're talking about.

(At which point, Randy Quigley, their supervisor, enters the office. The men immediately sit down and pretend to work. Quigley stops first at Charlie's desk.)

QUIGLEY: Krone, I need the Kimberly draft on my desk by noon. You got it? Big meeting.

CHARLIE: Yes sir.

QUIGLEY: Oh and by the way, tell your mother that she did a fine job picking out your tie today.

(Quigley laughs.)

CHARLIE: I'll tell her as soon as I get home, Mr. Quigley.

(Quigley laughs harder.)

QUIGLEY: Oh that's good! That's good. Well done, Krone.

(Quigley knocks his fist on Krone's desk in approval and moves to Tom's desk.)

QUIGLEY: *(Continued.)* Fineberg, you catch the game this weekend?

TOM: That new kid can really move on the base path, huh?

QUIGLEY: Like a rocket. He's a game changer, that guy. Listen, I need you to draft up a letter about the Clutsky deal.

TOM: No problem, Mr. Quigley.

QUIGLEY: That's what we like to hear.

(Quigley knocks on Tom's desk and moves to Spalding's desk.)

QUIGLEY: *(Continued.)* Spalding, I saw the mid-quarter earnings report. Your team's having a hell of a year, huh? I get close to this desk and I smell a promotion coming. Huh? Huh?

(Quigley laughs.)

SPALDING: Thank you, Mr. Quigley.

QUIGLEY: *(Louder so the other two guys can hear.)* And you know what that means . . . Team manager gets bumped, everybody gets a little bump bump.

(Tom and Krone give each other a high five. Quigley notices.)

QUIGLEY: *(Continued.)* Watch it, fellas. Quarter's not over yet.

(Quigley's about to head out, but he stops and looks Spalding over.)

QUIGLEY: *(Continued.)* You look pretty tired, Spalding. You get laid last night or something?

SPALDING: No. No I didn't, Mr. Quigley.

QUIGLEY: Yeah? Well why not?

(Charlie and Tom give a forced laugh along with Quigley.)

SPALDING: I suffer from bouts of impotence, due to my fennel allergy.

(All the men stop laughing.)

QUIGLEY: Oh. Well . . . I . . .

(Quigley doesn't know what to say, so he just leaves. Spalding goes back to work.)

(Charlie and Tom get up and approach Spalding quickly.)

CHARLIE: Dude. What was that?

SPALDING: What was what?

TOM: You just told the boss you've got impotence.

SPALDING: I know.

CHARLIE: Why?

SPALDING: Because of my fennel allergy.

TOM: No. Why'd you tell him that?

(A cloud washes over Spalding. Suddenly he realizes something's not quite right.)

SPALDING: I'm not sure.

CHARLIE: Well you'd better cut it out. They don't promote guys with impotence.

SPALDING: They don't?

CHARLIE: Of course they don't.

SPALDING: Oh.

TOM: You OK, man? You're acting really weird.

SPALDING: I don't know . . . I guess I just . . . forgot how to speak. I forgot what to say.

(Spalding looks up at them, a little panicked.)

SPALDING: *(Continued.)* Something must have happened, I must have hit my head or something . . .

CHARLIE: Look, Spalding, it's no big deal.

TOM: It's not?

CHARLIE: No, it's not. Everybody forgets essential life skills now and then. A couple years back I forgot how to shave. I've got the cream on my face, I've got the razor in my hand and I look down at it and I'm thinking: Now what the hell do I do with this thing?

SPALDING: Then what happened?

CHARLIE: I remembered.

TOM: Well either Spalding better remember, or we've got to remind him. You're never gonna get promoted, you keep talking like that. And if you don't get promoted . . .

SPALDING: You're right. I really don't know what's wrong with me. Maybe I have a headache.

TOM: Sure. A silent migraine, or something.

CHARLIE: I've read about that.

TOM: No big deal, it'll pass. Take some aspirin.

SPALDING: *(Smiling weakly.)* Right. You're right. I think I have some in my desk . . .

CHARLIE: So, Spalding, what'd you end up doing this weekend anyway?

SPALDING: Julie and I went to Westchester to visit her parents.

TOM: Oh man, the parents!

CHARLIE: There's your headache. How was it?

SPALDING: It was really nice. Julie's mom, Linda, made this gazpacho with just a touch of mint. It was lovely.

    (Pause.)

CHARLIE: Dude.

SPALDING: What?

CHARLIE: You can't say that.

SPALDING: Can't say what?

TOM: "Lovely." You can't use that word.

SPALDING: I can't? Why not?

CHARLIE: Because it's not a word you can use. It's like, an illegal word.

TOM: It's a woman word. Like: Aren't those panties lovely.

SPALDING: Oh. I see. *(Beat.)* But the gazpacho was lovely. It was full-bodied but still surprisingly delicate.

TOM: DUDE.

SPALDING: What?

CHARLIE: "Delicate."

SPALDING: I can't use *delicate* either?

TOM/CHARLIE: NO.

SPALDING: What words can I use?

TOM: You can use "good." You can say: Julie's mom made cold soup. It was good.

SPALDING: But it was more than good.

TOM: Then say it was very good.

SPALDING: But that doesn't really capture the complexity of it.

CHARLIE: It's soup. There's no "complexity." It's either good soup or bad soup. That's all there is.

SPALDING: That seems awfully limiting. To say that soup can only be good or bad implies that there's no middle ground. You're really dichotomizing soup.

(Beat.)

CHARLIE: I'm "dichotomizing" . . . ?

SPALDING: I just think there's more to soup than good or bad.

CHARLIE: It doesn't matter what you think. All that matters is how you say it. You can't say words like *lovely* and *delicate*. You sound like a pussy. You gotta pull it together man. Or that promotion is history.

SPALDING: You're right. Of course you're right. "Lovely gazpacho"? I don't know what's wrong with me today.

CHARLIE: It's no big deal. You're probably gonna snap out of it soon.

TOM: Long weekend away from the guys, maybe your brain got rewired or something. Don't worry. We'll fix it.

SPALDING: Thanks guys.

TOM: No problem, man.

CHARLIE: So, Westchester, huh? How'd you get out there?

SPALDING: We took the Saw Mill.

TOM: Yeah? How long did that take you?

SPALDING: Four hours.

CHARLIE: Four hours? That's a long time. Was there construction?

SPALDING: No.

TOM: An accident I bet.

SPALDING: No.

CHARLIE: Julie was nagging you to drive slow?

SPALDING: No she was asleep.

TOM: So what took you so long?

SPALDING: I like to drive slowly. *(Beat.)* Oh and there was this glorious vista. I stopped to take some pictures. *(Beat, the men stare at him.)* What? Oh. "Glorious." I can't use that word, right? Good. A good vista. No that doesn't really work. A great vista?

TOM: You can't use "vista" either.

SPALDING: Then what word am I supposed to use?

TOM: I don't know. Try "lookout."

SPALDING: But it wasn't really a lookout. I mean, yes, you could look out but that hardly captures the full magnitude of the view —

(Tom and Charlie exchange worried looks.)

TOM: Spalding, focus. OK, man? You wanna get better, you're gonna have to focus.

SPALDING: Right. Focus. OK. I'm sorry. Keep going.

CHARLIE: So, how long did it take you to get back?

SPALDING: I don't know. About an hour.

TOM: An hour? You made good time.

SPALDING: Yeah, Julie was driving.

(Tom and Charlie look at each other. Pause.)

TOM: *(To Charlie, deadly serious.)* Dude, what if this is contagious?

SPALDING: What'd I say wrong?

CHARLIE: *(To Tom.)* It's not.

TOM: How do you know? I mean, it could be some virus or something. Like the plague or something.

SPALDING: *(Worried.)* You think I have the plague?

CHARLIE: It's not the plague.

TOM: But how do you know that? What if we're risking our lives even breathing the same air as him? You know I can't come home talking like that. If I come home talking like that Jessica's out the door in five minutes. No man who talks like that can keep a girl like Jessica. I mean, you know that.

CHARLIE: I know. I know. Calm down. We're gonna fix him, OK?

(Charlie thinks about it for a second.)

I've got it. We just need a new approach. Tom, grab him.

TOM: I'm not touching him. What if he gives it to me?

CHARLIE: He's not gonna give it to you. Just grab him.

(Tom grabs Spalding's arms and pins them behind his back.)

SPALDING: Why are you grabbing me?

CHARLIE: Cause I'm gonna punch you in the stomach.

SPALDING: What?!

TOM: Don't worry, Spalding. It'll be good for you.

SPALDING: How will punching me in the stomach be good for me?!

CHARLIE: Trust me, man. That's one of your chick words isn't it, "trust"?

(Charlie and Tom laugh. Charlie tries for a shot, but Spalding is squirming around.)

SPALDING: Really guys. Thanks a lot but this isn't what I had in mind.

CHARLIE: *(Overlapping Spalding's lines.)* Tom, you gotta hold him still —

SPALDING: Maybe I just need to go away for a few days. Find some luxurious place —

(Charlie punches Spalding in the stomach.)

SPALDING: *(Continued.)* Owww! OK, not "luxurious." Someplace . . . splendid.

(Charlie punches Spalding in the stomach again.)

SPALDING: *(Continued.)* Tranquil.

(Tom, who doesn't mind this word, shrugs and lets Spalding go just as Charlie's punch lands in Tom's stomach.)

TOM: OW! What the hell was that for?

CHARLIE: Who told you to let him go?

TOM: I thought *tranquil* was OK!

CHARLIE: "Tranquil"? You think "tranquil's" OK?

(Tom thinks about it a moment.)

CHARLIE: *(Continued.)* I think it's OK.

(Tom grabs Spalding again.)

TOM: No, man, you're right. Let's go.

(Charlie punches him.)

SPALDING: What's wrong with *tranquil?* It evokes peacefulness and serenity —

(Another punch. And this time Charlie really hits him hard.)

SPALDING: *(Continued.)* STOP FUCKING PUNCHING ME YOU MEDIEVAL BASTARD!

(Enraged, Spalding shakes off Tom.)

TOM: Atta boy!!

(Tom slaps Spalding's ass.)

CHARLIE: Well done, Spalding!

(Charlie playfully bodychecks Spalding. Spalding puts his hands on his knees and takes deep breaths.)

CHARLIE: *(Continued.)* Now. How do you feel?

SPALDING: *(Spalding takes a couple rasping breaths before speaking.)* Emotionally lost and isolated.

(Tom and Charlie groan.)

TOM: Come on man! How about angry? How 'bout pissed off? You feel angry Spalding?

SPALDING: Well, yes . . .

CHARLIE: OK, so punch me back. Come on, punch me back.

SPALDING: What would that accomplish?

CHARLIE: It'll make you feel better about yourself.

SPALDING: I'd really just rather talk about why you felt the need to express your concern for me through physical violence.

TOM: *(Getting fed up.)* Man, you've gotta stop talking like that.

SPALDING: Like what?

TOM: Like using so many words! Describing things!

SPALDING: But if I can't describe things how am I supposed to convey how they make me feel?

CHARLIE: You're not!

SPALDING: I'm not supposed to convey how I'm feeling?

TOM: NO. You're not supposed to feel.

SPALDING: *(Laughs.)* But that's ridiculous. If I'm not supposed to feel then how can I ever be truly alive? How can I fully experience the entire range of human experience?

CHARLIE: The same way every other guy does. Through sports.

SPALDING: But sports engender competition and aggression.

TOM: Yeah. That's why we like them.

CHARLIE: Listen, Spalding, you gotta pull it together. You gotta get normal or all our asses are on the line.

TOM: Seriously, man . . .

SPALDING: I know. I know. I'm sorry.

CHARLIE: It's OK. It's OK. OK, Spalding, try this: Hey, Tom, you catch the ball game last night?

TOM: That new pitcher can really throw.

CHARLIE: Spalding, what'd you think of the new pitcher?

SPALDING: I don't know. I didn't watch the game.

CHARLIE: Yeah but still. You're supposed to know. You're supposed to have an opinion.

SPALDING: I'm supposed to have an opinion about something I know nothing about?

CHARLIE/TOM: YES.

SPALDING: Why?

TOM: Because you're a man.

SPALDING: Oh. OK. OK. I'll give it a try.

CHARLIE: So. Spalding, what'd you think of the new kid?

SPALDING: He had some beautiful pitches. Really inspiring.

TOM: Oh come on man —

SPALDING: Sorry. They were good pitches. Really good.

CHARLIE: And what about the other team?

SPALDING: The other team? Oh. They were bad. Really bad.

CHARLIE: OK, you're doing fine.

SPALDING: Our team was good and the other team was bad.

TOM: OK, you got it.

CHARLIE: *(Changing tactics.)* Hey, you guys see the new girl in accounting?

TOM: Yeah she's pretty hot.

SPALDING: Yeah. She's good.

TOM: Not like Fat Melanie in legal.

SPALDING: Fat Melanie. She's bad.

TOM: OK Spalding, you got it. Now you can move on to other words.

SPALDING: Which other words?

CHARLIE: You know, like: hot or ugly.

SPALDING: OK.

TOM: Right or wrong.

CHARLIE: Good or evil.

TOM: Nice or bitchy. Are you getting it?

SPALDING: I think so. I think I am.

TOM: What do you think about Charlie's mom?

SPALDING: Charlie's mom's ugly.

CHARLIE: What do you think about Tom's wife?

SPALDING: Tom's wife's a bitch.

TOM: *(Suddenly serious.)* What'd you say about my wife?

SPALDING: I said she's a bitch.

TOM: You can't talk like that about somebody's wife.

SPALDING: Why not? She is a bitch.

> *(Tom punches Spalding in the head.)*

CHARLIE: Hey, c'mon guys —

> *(Spalding sinks to the floor, dizzy.)*

TOM: Oh man, I'm sorry, I didn't mean to —

SPALDING: *(Standing up.)* No, it's OK.

CHARLIE: You OK, Spalding?

SPALDING: Yeah. Yeah. Of course I'm OK. What're you kidding? Pussy punch like that? I'm fine.

> *(Tom and Charlie stare at Spalding.)*

SPALDING: *(Continued.)* What're all we doing, standing around like a bunch of assholes? I think it's time to get back to work, don't you? Let's go. Move.

> *(Tom and Charlie look at Spalding, surprised. Then they smile and nod.)*

TOM/CHARLIE: No problem boss. Well done. To work we go.

SPALDING: Oh and Tom, your wife really is a bitch. But she's hot, so it's OK.

TOM: Thanks, man.

> *(As the guys go back to work, Quigley enters the office. He approaches Spalding.)*

SPALDING: Hey there, Mr. Quigley.

QUIGLEY: Spalding. What'd you do this weekend?

SPALDING: Went to Westchester to see Julie's parents.

QUIGLEY: Oh. Rough.

SPALDING: Yeah. It was pretty bad.

QUIGLEY: How'd you get out there?

SPALDING: We took the Saw Mill.

QUIGLEY: How long did it take you?

SPALDING: Four hours.

QUIGLEY: Traffic?

SPALDING: No. Julie was nagging me to drive slow.

QUIGLEY: Ah. How long did it take you to get back?

SPALDING: Just under an hour.

QUIGLEY: That's good time.

SPALDING: I know. I knocked Julie out.

(Quigley and Spalding laugh. Quigley pounds Spalding on the back.)

QUIGLEY: You know Spalding, I think you're gonna do just fine in this company. Just fine.

(Spalding and Quigley walk offstage, laughing, chatting.)

SPALDING: Thanks, Mr. Quigley.

(Spalding and Quigley exit. Charlie looks over at Tom, they sigh in relief and then go back to work.)

END OF PLAY

Remind Me Again

A ten-minute encounter for the stage

Sharyn Rothstein

Remind Me Again was originally produced at the Ensemble Studio Theatre in New York in June, 2003. It was directed by Tara Merdjanoff. The cast was as follows: Miranda: Jennie McClintock; Jane: Erin Andrea; Suze: Shani Petroff; KissyInvader: Jeremy Bohen.

CHARACTERS
Three young professional women:
MIRANDA, conservatively dressed
JANE, a little flashy
SUZE, pink and married
. . . and the KISSYINVADER, a nondescript man

SETTING
Scene One: A city street corner
Scene Two: A beige corporate office — kitchen

• • •

SCENE ONE

Miranda, a young professional in workday wardrobe, walks though the park on her way to the office. The birds are tweeting, the sun is shining, sex is always consensual, and cookies are good for you.

Suddenly, a man — KissyInvader — his face obscured by passing people or our perspective — knocks into Miranda.

Just as Miranda looks up at him KissyInvader, whose back should be to the audience and who should be of a nondescript nature, leans down and almost kisses her.

Miranda steps back, frozen in shock.

KissyInvader laughs loudly and heads off into the park — just another pedestrian.

Miranda, floored, smoothes out her hair, her blouse, tries to catch her breath, and walks off.

SCENE TWO

Miranda rushes into her office's beige, corporate kitchen, shaken. Jane, Miranda's coworker, a well-dressed, hard-looking, know-it-all type, is pouring herself coffee.

MIRANDA: Hey — Jane: Listen to this: I'm walking down the street this morning, I look up, and some guy almost kisses me. Can you believe that?
JANE: Oh my God.
MIRANDA: I know!

JANE: That's fantastic! Was he hot?

MIRANDA: I don't know — I wasn't really paying attention —. I don't know if he was "hot." And I really don't think it matters. What matters is that he completely invaded my space — he —

JANE: Well, yeah, but would you care so much if he was a good-looking man invading your space?

MIRANDA: Yes!

JANE: Bullshit.

MIRANDA: I can't even believe you're arguing this.

JANE: Look. Suze, from the third floor?, met her husband because he "invaded her space." They were on the subway and he grabbed her breasts and said, "These are lovely."

MIRANDA: He grabbed her breasts?

JANE: Uh huh.

MIRANDA: And she married him?

JANE: Yes. But the point is that he had the courage to say something to her. And that he's attractive, because if he wasn't attractive then it would've just been another case of, you know, sexual harassment or something. *(Suze, late twenties, in a much-planned pink outfit, sashays into the kitchen to refill her coffee.)*

JANE: *(Continued.)* Suze! I was just telling Miranda how you met Mark! *(Suze swats Jane in a girly way.)*

SUZE: Oh my God! Isn't it a gas?

MIRANDA: It's —

SUZE: You know, I'd gotten so used to scowling at every man who said something to me that I almost completely blew it. But something stopped me. I turned, fully prepared to scowl, but then I just . . . smiled. I like to think that it was because of fate. Or because he's white.

MIRANDA: Because he's white?

SUZE: You better believe it. Like an albino.

MIRANDA: *(A little grossed out.)* Oh.

JANE: Some guy tried to kiss Miranda on the street today.

SUZE: *(Continued.)* Oh! How wonderful for you!

JANE: Miranda considers it an invasion of privacy.

SUZE: Well, I guess . . . but isn't it romantic?

MIRANDA: No, I really don't think it is.

SUZE: *(Looking at Jane knowingly.)* Oh.

MIRANDA: What?

SUZE: He wasn't attractive, was he?

MIRANDA: I don't — I don't know! Why does it matter if he was attractive or not?

SUZE: Ohhhh. I get it. Was he black?

MIRANDA: I don't know!

JANE: How can you not know?

MIRANDA: I wasn't really paying attention — I was so shocked — I don't remember what race he was.

SUZE: Oh. Then he was probably Puerto Rican. They can be kind of ambiguous.

MIRANDA: Ambiguous? This isn't — look, the point is, this man — a stranger — someone I don't know, leaned down, tried to kiss me, then laughed and walked away. I'm so — look at me, I'm shaking! I'm completely shaken up.

(Beat.)

JANE: Oh. You didn't tell me he laughed.

MIRANDA: Does it matter? Either way—

JANE: Well, of course it matters.

SUZE: Yeah. Laughing is rude.

MIRANDA: The whole thing is rude!

SUZE: Yeah, but laughing? It's like . . . They only laugh if they think you're really ugly.

JANE: Or fat.

SUZE: You know, because then it's a joke.

JANE: Because then you're a joke. *(Short pause.)* Don't you think?

MIRANDA: I — *(They look at her.)* I guess. I didn't really think about the laugh—

SUZE: Yeah. It probably affected you on an inner level. Laughing can really make you insecure.

(Suze and Jane nod at each other.)

MIRANDA: Look, the laugh didn't — the whole thing made me insecure. That guy made me insecure. I mean it just left me dumbfounded. How can a human being treat another human being with such . . . such disrespect?

JANE: Well, why didn't you ask him?

MIRANDA: Ask him?

JANE: Sure. I mean, he was about to kiss you, you might as well ask why, don't you think?

MIRANDA: Well, I — I didn't really think I could ask him. I thought he might, you know, if I said something he might get . . . violent.

SUZE: *(Nodding to Jane.)* Definitely Puerto Rican.

JANE: Really, Miranda. It was the middle of the day. He's not going to rape you in the middle of the day.

MIRANDA: He's not?

JANE: No. Besides, rapists don't bother women during the day.

MIRANDA: They don't?

JANE: Why would they? It goes against their entire plan of action. If you harass a woman when she's walking around by herself in the middle of the day she's going to be that much less likely to walk around by herself at night, when it's easy to rape her.

SUZE: That's true.

JANE: Rapists are nocturnal. Like hedgehogs.

MIRANDA: Hedgehogs?

JANE: Yes. Many people don't know that hedgehogs are nocturnal. And like hedgehogs, rapists are creatures that, while very vulnerable within, have evolved, due to the demands of Mother Nature, into prickly, aloof animals. *(Short pause.)* You can't touch a hedgehog . . .

SUZE: Just like how you can't touch a rapist.

(Beat/Pause.)

MIRANDA: Why would you want to touch a rapist?

(Suze and Jane look at her.)

SUZE: We're speaking metaphorically Miranda.

JANE: Look, so the guy "invaded your space," so he "intruded on your privacy." At least it was real.

MIRANDA: Real?

JANE: Think about how few really real experiences we have in our lives. How few personal interactions we have with others.

SUZE: It's a blessing.

JANE: It is.

SUZE: It's how I met Mark.

JANE: And he's an albino.

MIRANDA: *(Growing increasingly frenzied.)* So you're saying, when a man — any man — walks by you on the street and, and calls something out: "hey baby" "nice ass, gimme a smile" anything . . . it doesn't bother you? It doesn't make you anxious?

JANE/SUZE: No.

MIRANDA: You're saying if someone grabbed you on the street and just — like this —

(Miranda, in a bit of a frenzy, grabs Jane's face, almost kisses her and then laughs. She lets go. An awkward pause.)

MIRANDA: *(Continued.) (Embarrassed.)* That doesn't make you uncomfortable?

JANE: Well of course that made me uncomfortable. You're a woman. *(Suze and Jane exchange disapproving nods. Beat.)* And we're in an office.

SUZE: Really, Miranda. There's a time and place for everything.

MIRANDA: That's . . . I don't understand. So a man . . . On the street . . . doesn't make you uncomfortable? Do most women feel this way?

SUZE: I can't really speak for most women, Miranda. I believe in the individual.

MIRANDA: Jane?

JANE: Yes, I think they do, Miranda. And do you want to know why?

MIRANDA: Please.

JANE: Alright. *(A dramatic pause.)* Come with me on a journey of the mind. Imagine the last time you awoke in the morning, shaved your legs, blew out your hair, slipped into a stunning new outfit, walked out on the street and . . . not a single man said anything.

(Suze and Miranda gasp an agonized gasp.)

JANE: *(Continued.)* Exactly. You can't pick and choose. Either you want male attention or you don't.

MIRANDA: But it shouldn't be all or nothing!

JANE: Look Miranda, you can't be reliant on men one day and disgusted by them the next. You'd go totally bipolar.

SUZE: Noah only let the animals on in twosies, Miranda. If you try to walk alone, you'll just drown in the flood.

MIRANDA: *(Trying to understand Suze's remark.)* Well, but . . . but . . . I mean, doesn't it scare you? The idea that at any moment any man could just — just say something to you, say something about you? Touch you? Follow you?

JANE: Miranda, you have to be realistic. Look at Mindy, from the fourth floor? Three years ago, a man told her had a hot ass and she stopped going out at night, threw out all her mini skirts, and completely stopped waxing her upper lip.

SUZE: *(Nodding.)* She went totally Hasidic.

MIRANDA: She did?

JANE: And did it help? Did it change the world? Did it change one single man? No.

SUZE: No.

MIRANDA: *(Hopelessly.)* No.

JANE: No.

SUZE: No.

MIRANDA: *(A sad realization.)* No.

JANE: So I mean why not embrace it? Why not enjoy it? Enjoy the catcalling, the name calling, the ass grabbing. Enjoy being stared at, pawed at, mauled in public. Enjoy holding your keys between your fingers at night, carrying mace in your sports bra when you jog. *(Becoming frenzied.)* Enjoy darting back and forth from one side of the road to the other just because a MAN is coming toward you. *(Beat.)* I mean, enjoy it. *(Short pause.)* I know I do.

MIRANDA: You do?

JANE: Yes, I do. *(Beat.)* It reminds me that I'm a woman. *(Beat.)* And aren't I lucky?

(Jane and Suze smile at each other gaily. They look at Miranda expectantly. Miranda smiles weakly. Jane and Suze exit, chatting, leaving Miranda alone on stage, her smile fading.)

END OF PLAY

Hell Hath Three Furies

AOISE STRATFORD

CHARACTERS

    MACA: Film noir hero/villain in love with the wrong dame(s)

    BETH: his wife, an obsessive cook (also one of Hell's Furies of torment)

    JULIET: his shrink, darkly romantic (also one of Hell's Furies of torment)

    HEATHER: his mistress, a femme fatale (also one of Hell's Furies of torment)

CASTING NOTE

    Actors should be age in the range twenties to thirties and can be of any ethnicity.

SETTING

    A couch in Hell

TIME

    Eternity . . . or about 1950

• • •

In silhouette a tableau: Mac is seated on a couch, the only piece of furniture in an otherwise empty space. The three Furies who will also become Beth (his wife), Juliet (his shrink), and Heather (his mistress) are posed like 1940's femme fatales around him. Mac lifts his hat, a salute to the audience, and then he addresses the audience. The Furies act as a chorus, sometimes speaking together or individually, to the audience, to him, or to each other until taking on their named characters:

MAC: Welcome to Hell. I know what you're thinking, but when I say Hell, I mean Hell. Look, I'm not a bad guy . . . but one wrong turn and now I'm stuck here with these dames. The fates; the three Furies.

FURIES: Poor thing. Someone should have told him bad luck comes in threes.

MAC: I'll be straight with you. I murdered my wife. Shot her. I probably shouldn't have done that. But she's a broad that can really make a man crazy. And I almost got away with it.

FURIES: Almost.

MAC: If it weren't for my shrink: Crazy dame threatened to blow the whistle on me so I had to take her out too. I didn't want to . . . I didn't even mean to.

FURIES: Excuse me?

MAC: OK, I meant to. But I regret it now. I wish my prints weren't on that gun. I wish I didn't have their blood on my hands. I get a little crazy if I don't take my pills. And the worst part is, when I was arrested, my girlfriend Heather /

FURIES: Died of a broken heart?

MAC: Yes. But I wish you'd all shut up and let me tell the story my way. *(Beat.)* I could really use a break here. A second chance. If only I could . . .

FURIES: What? Go back in time? Do things differently? Follow another path?

MAC: Is that crazy?

FURIES: Don't ask me, Mac, I'm not your shrink.

MAC: I mean, that's sometimes the only thing a guy wants. To turn back the clock. Right now, I've got three dead women on my tail, but if I could just go back and put the gun someplace safe, call things off, straighten up. What am I saying. There's never any going back, is there? *(A beat.)*

FURIES: Maybe. Maybe not. Maybe just this once.

(The Furies blow Mac a kiss, blowing him off the couch and out of the scene.)
(Beth [one of the Furies] comes forward and addresses the audience.)

BETH: Mac loves my brownies. He used to say one of my brownies and three pills got him out of bed on the right side. We have a nice bedroom suite, and I sometimes joke with Mac that when your life is so pretty there is no wrong side to get out of. We have a nice house. Mac has a nice face. There is rat poison in these. I've never tried making them like this before. Lately, I sometimes see Mac staring at me like he wishes I was someone else. The other day he said "Shove your Goddam carrot cake up your ass." I think today Mac and I will each have a brownie and then things will be better.

FURIES: *(Announcing the "scene" to the audience.)* One kind of Hell. Brownies are a weapon.

MAC: Hi Honey, I'm home

BETH: You're late.

MAC: I know. I'm sorry.

BETH: I forgive you. Brownie? Dinner's burnt.

MAC: I said sorry.

BETH: Charcoal casserole.

MAC: Beth, for God's sakes.

BETH: Maybe I should stick my head in the oven.

MAC: *(To the audience.)* See my problem?

BETH: But we don't have gas.

MAC: *(Pulls gun.)* You know, if you weren't such a nagging crackpot, maybe I wouldn't be about to do this. *(A beat.)* Wait. I thought I was going to get rid of this thing; avoid temptation. I better go see Juliet before I do something stupid.

(The "scene" ends, Beth and Mac move away or freeze. Juliet (the second Fury) steps forward and talks to the audience:)

JULIET: I became a doctor because I wanted a big office with a smooth chrome desk and lots of pencils in a jar. Sharp pencils. And a view of the park and a lock on the door. I like to watch the trees change color, I think that's very healthy, don't you? I keep jelly beans and valium in my drawer for special occasions, like when my patients are good. Though really, my favorite patients are bad, and that's just the way I like 'em.

FURIES: *(Announcing the "scene" to the audience.)* What Happens on The Love Seat.

JULIET: You're late.

MAC: I know. I'm sorry. I was walking . . . thinking.

JULIET: Don't apologize, Mac. You're always late. I still bill you by the hour.

MAC: That's not a very supportive thing to say, Doc.

JULIET: Oh, Schnookums. I've told you, call me Juliet.

MAC: As you point out, Juliet, I pay by the hour. I'd like my money's worth. Or rather, my wife's money's worth. I almost didn't come today but I need your help.

JULIET: Mac. Sit. Let me take poor baby's worries away

MAC: I've run out of pills and it's making me crazy.

JULIET: Well I can't just go handing out drugs, Mac, that just wouldn't be responsible now, would it? Besides, I like you a little crazy.

MAC: I've been thinking of killing my wife. I see it in my head, just like it's real. There's all this blood. I know I shouldn't do it but . . . See my problem?

JULIET: Fascinating. Let's talk about why you want your wife dead.

MAC: She's an ogre. But she's rich. And I want to run off to Florida with someone else.

JULIET: Three excellent motives. And this someone else . . . Have anyone in mind?

MAC: Yes. Heather. She's a doll. And she'd do anything for me.

JULIET: Anything?

MAC: Well sometimes when I ask her to do stuff . . . never mind. But about killing my wife . . . I can't do it. Or can I? I want to, but one wrong turn can finish a man in this town. It's a terrible dilemma. I feel like that famous Shakespeare character, you know?

JULIET: Hamlet?

MAC: No. The other one. So I have three requests.

JULIET: Shoot.

MAC: Actually, that's what I'd like to avoid.

JULIET: So what do you want from me?

MAC: Firstly, keep this meeting confidential; if anyone asks, I was never here. Secondly, look after this for me. *(Hands over the gun.)* And thirdly, can I have a jelly bean?

JULIET: Anything you want, Sweet Pea.

(The "scene" ends. Heather [the third Fury] comes forward to talk to the audience:)

HEATHER: I've never been to Florida. They say the moon there is made of gold and the stars are diamonds. I can't wait to see that. A girl has to choose her man carefully. It's a tough world but some of us weren't built for tough, if you catch my drift. Mac better not let me down. I've bought a new bikini. He can be a little soft sometimes, but I know how to harden him up. *(She is passed a phone by one of the Furies. She calls Mac.)* Hi Sweetie.

FURIES: *(Announcing the "scene" to the audience.)* To Flee or Not to Flee.

MAC: *(He is also passed a phone, then.)* Heather.

HEATHER: All ready for the big trip?

MAC: I . . . ah . . . I think we need to talk.

HEATHER: We can talk all you like over pina coladas in Miami. Oh, Mac. Do you suppose they have those there? I mean, they have coconuts don't they? And what else are you supposed to do with a coconut?

MAC: I don't know.

HEATHER: Mac, you're not going to disappoint me, are you?

MAC: Well . . .

HEATHER: Mac. Sweetie. Get it together. Kisses. *(Hangs up. Then to the audience.)* By tomorrow, Mac and I will be on a plane to Florida. I might be trouble, but I'm worth it.

FURIES: *(Announcing the "scene" to the audience.)* Single Gun Theory (or) Be Careful What You Wish For.

(Beth is baking brownies, she holds a pan. There is the sound of a knock at the door. Beth looks in the wrong direction. Heather enters.)

BETH: Oh. Hello. Brownie?

HEATHER: What?

BETH: Fresh from the oven!

HEATHER: No. I don't want a brownie. Where's Mac?

BETH: Not here, but he'll be home soon. He's always /

HEATHER: Late. Yes. I know. He was supposed to meet me at the airport just now, but he stood me up and I just can't have him changing his mind like that. I mean; I've packed already.

BETH: I'm his wife, Beth. So who are you, dear?

HEATHER: Your worst nightmare.

BETH: Really? Well that's odd. My worst nightmare involves this guy in a big cape with sunglasses and blond hair and thigh high boots and a whip and . . . oh, no hang on, that's not the nightmare /
(Heather takes out a knife and goes to stab her.)

BETH: No! Wait!

HEATHER: What now?
(Beth runs behind the couch quickly eats a brownie and dies, falling out of sight.)

HEATHER: *(Continued.)* Oh. Well that's handy. Mac can be as indecisive as a two-headed snake. He was never going to leave her. Now he doesn't have to.
(A knock at the door Heather looks in the wrong direction. Juliet enters with Mac's gun.)

HEATHER: Oh. Hello.

JULIET: I've always wondered what you'd look like.

HEATHER: I'm sorry?

JULIET: Mac never said. Is he here? I came as soon as I could.

HEATHER: Mac? No he's not here. Not yet.

JULIET: Oh good, I'm just in time then. Thank God we can rely on Mac to wander around thinking for half an hour before keeping appointments.

HEATHER: Who are you?

JULIET: Your worst nightmare.

HEATHER: *(To the audience.)* That sounds kind of familiar. So it's about now that I'm tipped off that this is not going to go so well for me.
(Juliet shoots her.)

JULIET: *(Turning her head to face the audience.)* Bang.

HEATHER: You bitch.
(Heather dies. Drops the knife.)

JULIET: *(To the audience.)* Well don't look surprised. You know what they say about the theater, you can't have a gun without a body.
(A knock at the door. Mac enters.)

MAC: Hi honey, I'm . . . Oh my God, Doc. What are you doing here?

JULIET: You said she'd do anything for you. But you were wrong.

MAC: What?

JULIET: I, on the other hand, really would do anything. Anything. I know what you want, what you need, and I'm just mad enough to take the necessary actions. It's your lucky day, Mac. I love you.

MAC: Oh my God. Is that a dagger I /

JULIET: Isn't Schnookums glad I killed his nasty old wifie for him?

MAC: That is not my wife. That's my girlfriend, Heather.

JULIET: That's Heather? But this is your house. What the hell is she doing here?

MAC: And where the hell is my wife, Beth?

JULIET: Don't worry about that, Mac, it's just you and me now.

MAC: Forget it, Juliet: I could never love a twisted broad like you.

JULIET: Oh, shit. *(Tiny beat.)* Really?

(Mac just rolls his eyes.)

JULIET: *(Continued.)* Damn; that was a waste of effort. And my prints are all over that thing. Oh, well. *(Seeing the knife.)* I guess there's just one way out. Oh, happy dagger! Let me die . . .

(Juliet stabs herself. A beat. Mac sits on the couch, the same position he was in at the opening. The women are dead around him.)

MAC: *(To the audience.)* So all roads really do lead to Rome and I guess someone down here wants me wearing a toga. Regret's a sharp-toothed dog and no mistake. And I got bit three times.

(Slowly the women rise again, resuming their opening tableau. Beth holds the tray of brownies.)

FURIES: Poor thing. Someone should have told him. You can't outrun fate. And you don't have to pull the trigger to be guilty. Welcome to Hell, Mac. Brownie?

(Blackout.)

END OF PLAY

A Moment of Your Undivided Attention

ALINA TROWBRIDGE

CHARACTERS

MONA: forty-five, feminine, dressed for a formal party: neck, shoulder, cleavage in evidence

EMILIA: Mona's sidekick; same age, also dressed formally, but no skin exposed; businesslike

JACK O'CONNOR: Mona's ex-husband; fiftyish, exuding the health reclaimed from overwork that comes with power and a classy gym membership

CASS: O'Connor's new wife; twenty-seven. The girl knows how to wear a dress

SETTING

An urban high-rise

•   •   •

A formal evening party in an urban high-rise. Cass and O'Connor sit on a love seat, holding wine glasses. There's an empty chair on each side of the love seat. Cass glances around the room. O'Connor fastens his eyes on her.

O'CONNOR: Who are you looking for?

CASS: No one. Just curious about who's here.

O'CONNOR: Don't look around the room. It makes us look weak. Let them find us, come to us.

(Mona and Emilia enter.)

CASS: Who is that woman?

O'CONNOR: What did I say. Don't look around the room.

CASS: *(Looking at O'Connor at the level of his necktie.)* Fine. She's just a striking woman, that's all. A lot of people are looking. *(O'Connor looks.)*

O'CONNOR: Damn it to hell.

CASS: You know her? A business rival.

O'CONNOR: Straight for us. When they get here, don't stand up.

(Mona and Emilia walk to O'Connor and Cass, Emilia following Mona. This puts Cass between Mona and O'Connor.)

MONA: O'Connor. Why are you still alive?

O'CONNOR: I've always had excellent survival instincts.

MONA: Is that the new buzz word for bullying? And who is your friend?

(Mona extends her hand to Cass. Cass stands to take it.)

CASS: Cass O'Connor. I'm Jack's wife.

MONA: I'm Mona. Jack's first wife. And this is my friend, Emilia Hammond. You've heard of her, of course.

(Emilia crosses to O'Connor's other side and extends a hand. Now he is obliged to stand up. Also to turn slightly away from Mona and Cass.)

EMILIA: I know. Shaking hands is meant to be friendly, but it puts people at a distance. So formal. The Romans did it to check each other for weapons.

O'CONNOR: It's a pleasure, of course. I had no idea Mona knew you.

EMILIA: Oh, Mona has been promising to introduce us for ages.

MONA: How long have you and O'Connor been married?

EMILIA: There are a number of things you and I ought to discuss.

CASS: You call your ex-husband by his last name?

MONA: Like high school boys. A pleasant mix of familiarity and emotional distance.

EMILIA: I think there are some very promising subjects for conversation between us.

O'CONNOR: You have an impressive track record.

MONA: So, how long?

CASS: A year. You must have seen it in the papers.

O'CONNOR: But I have quite a few projects going already.

EMILIA: Who said anything about another project? I said conversation. I was talking about talk.

MONA: Tell me. How many times has he hit you so far?

(A break in the chatter. O'Connor hasn't quite heard, but he senses something's wrong.)

EMILIA: It's a party, Mr. O'Connor. Surely you can take a break from work for two hours together.

O'CONNOR: I would if everyone else would.

CASS: Why did you say that? Why would you say something so bizarre?

MONA: A year. By now, you should have graduated to a full beating.

EMILIA: If you think I'm that dangerous, perhaps I'd better move on.

MONA: At least a good pummeling. Below the sternum, where it won't show.

EMILIA: There's Preston Roberts by the balcony. He won't be afraid of a little casual conversation.

O'CONNOR: No, but he's as boring as hell.

MONA: Pinned between the wall and his fist so there's no room for the rebound. The sound of your own ribs cracking.

O'CONNOR: You wouldn't even enjoy kicking his ass.

MONA: A sudden twist of the arm, harder, then harder, always somehow short of actually breaking it.

EMILIA: What makes you think I want to kick his ass?

O'CONNOR: Anyone who reads the financial pages knows that.

MONA: Perhaps you've already experienced the curious sensation of being held upside down by your ankle and having your head banged on the floor.

O'CONNOR: And I know considerably more than anyone who reads the financial pages.

MONA: The bumps wouldn't show under all that lovely hair.

O'CONNOR: But my plate is full. I'm not your guy.

CASS: You don't understand.

MONA: He chose the dress for you, didn't he? Perfectly designed to show your lovely neck while exactly covering the bruises.

EMILIA: You think I'm about to make a mistake. Don't you? You're wrong, you know. Wrong.

CASS: Him. You don't understand him.

MONA: Right. You never speak of it.

O'CONNOR: Sometimes it's easier to see the field when you're playing a different game.

MONA: Because he didn't mean it.

EMILIA: I've got my money on the right horse, Mr. O'Connor.

MONA: Because he was drunk.

EMILIA: I think you'd enjoy the race.

CASS: He can't control his emotions.

EMILIA: We don't exactly need you. But it would make things so much more interesting.

CASS: He's sorry afterward.

MONA: How do you know? Does he say so?

EMILIA: And so much more lucrative.

CASS: When you love someone, you deal with things. You wait for them to get better.

O'CONNOR: If things turn out the way you think they will.

EMILIA: They always do.

MONA: I'm on your side and you're on his. I knew it would be this way.

O'CONNOR: Famous last words.

MONA: Listen, here are the rules. Never leave the house without your own keys.

EMILIA: You think you know something.

O'CONNOR: I hear things that make me wonder.

MONA: Never leave the house without your cell phone and enough cash for a motel room.

O'CONNOR: Preston Roberts.

EMILIA: Careful.

CASS: Please stop talking to me.

MONA: Tell someone you trust so you have somewhere to run.

CASS: Please stop now.

O'CONNOR: And Ashton Craig.

EMILIA: In this business, they put people in jail for knowing something.

CASS: I need to go to the ladies' room. *(Turning.)* Jack, please excuse me. I need to find the ladies' room.

O'CONNOR: *(Privately to Cass.)* Wait a little longer. Don't abandon the field to them.

CASS: I don't feel well.

O'CONNOR: Show some guts, for a change. Why the hell can't you ever show any guts.

MONA: I need to freshen up, myself. Let's go look for the ladies' room together.

CASS: That's all right. I can wait.

EMILIA: Is there any such thing as a drink around here?

O'CONNOR: They came by a few minutes ago.

CASS: I'll get them.

O'CONNOR: They'll come by again.

> *(Emilia sits down. So does Mona. O'Connor and Cass both find themselves facing people several feet below them. Reluctantly, they sit.)*

MONA: I'm afraid your new wife doesn't like me very much, O'Connor.

O'CONNOR: *(Patting Cass' knee.)* I'm sure that's not true. You're exaggerating. *(Gripping Cass' knee.)* You always exaggerate. *(Cass flinches.)*

MONA: That would be a waste of imagination. The truth is hard enough to believe without exaggerating.

O'CONNOR: I'm afraid your friend didn't get what she was after.

MONA: Those survival instincts of yours.

O'CONNOR: Like I said.

MONA: I think you'll find that Emilia always gets what she's after.

EMILIA: *(Standing.)* Unfortunately, Mona and I have another party to get to.

MONA: *(Also standing.)* So much to say, so little time.

> *(O'Connor again finds himself obliged to stand. Cass remains seated.)*

MONA: *(To Cass.)* Good-bye, Cass. Perhaps we'll talk another time.

EMILIA: *(Shaking hands with O'Connor.)* So nice to chat with you, Mr. O'Connor. Mrs. O'Connor.

MONA: I've been told that giving up the field is giving up power. But this time, I think that isn't so. Good night, O'Connor.

> *(Mona and Emilia exit, slowly. O'Connor sits down. He drinks his wine.)*

END OF PLAY

PLAYS FOR
FIVE ACTORS

Tina at the *Times*
or
Below the Fold

WENDY MACLEOD

CHARACTERS

TINA: new editor of the *Times*, glamorous, possible English accent
JEREMY: Tina's assistant
TIM: editor, International section
MELISSA: Science editor
DARREN: Arts and Leisure editor

SETTING

The *Times* office

. . .

Tina sits at the head of a conference table, a telephone with many buttons in front of her. Around the table sit Tim, the senior editor of the International section, Melissa, the Science Editor, and Darren, the Arts and Leisure editor. Jeremy, Tina's handsome, dandyish assistant, stands behind her chair with a cell phone in his pocket. Offstage, there is a dolly and file cabinet.

TINA: All right ladies and gentlemen, page one! International, what have you got?

TIM: We've been looking at the Honduran relief efforts, apparently the relief supplies are not getting through; they're being warehoused and sold by corrupt government officials at the local levels . . .

TINA: Are you saying that we send off our little shoeboxes filled with toothpaste and tube socks and the poor people never get them?

TIM: Exactly.

TINA: I can see the headline CLOSE YOUR CHECKBOOKS!

TIM: People shouldn't close their checkbooks but the U.S. Government needs to . . .

TINA: The U.S. Government, don't talk to me about Washington, have you seen what they *wear* down there?

TIM: The article's not suggesting that charity's a waste of time . . . .

TINA: CHARITY A WASTE OF TIME! Get me a mock up. Science, what have you got?

MELISSA: We have a piece on global warming . . .

TINA: The weather! Fabulous!

MELISSA: The polar ice cap normally melts at a rate of an inch every ten years, but in the last five years it's melted . . .

TINA: Statistics! What did I tell you about statistics, my love?

MELISSA: Well they can be skewed of course . . .

TINA: Boring!

MELISSA: We're just trying to illustrate that . . .

TINA: Good. What's the photo?

MELISSA: I brought some possibilities . . . .

(Tina glances at them.)

TINA: Ice? An iceberg? Please. Too white.

MELISSA: But . . .

TINA: Not after Labor Day!

(The intercom buzzes.)

INTERCOM: Edward R. Murrow to see you.

TINA: Who?

INTERCOM: Edward R . . .

TINA: Meeting!

(She buzzes out.)

I think my point is why should we care?

MELISSA: The krill are dying . . .

TINA: And the krill are . . . ?

MELISSA: They're like little shrimp . . .

TINA: Oh, *shrimp* . . . *(To Jeremy.)* book me a table for 8:00, my love.

(Jeremy begins dialing and murmuring a dinner reservation into a cell phone.)

MELISSA: It's what the penguins eat, the whales . . .

TINA: Well the whales could stand to stand to lose a few . . .

MELISSA: But if they die . . .

TINA: Exactly if they die who cares? A bunch of Eskimos?

JEREMY: Inuits.

TINA: Is there any film potential here?

MELISSA: Ummm . . .

TINA: *(As if Melissa is an idiot.)* Can — this — article — turn — into — a — book — which — will — be — sold — to — the — movies?

MELISSA: Maybe if somebody had to *save* the polar ice cap . . .

JEREMY: Keanu Reeves.

MELISSA: Like if Keanu Reeves had to fly into space and fix the hole in the ozone . . .

TINA: What's the ticking clock?

MELISSA: I'm sorry?

TINA: What happens if he doesn't fix it in a certain amount of time?

MELISSA: The krill die?

TINA: Maybe if Kim Basinger played the krill. Get me the Hollywood angle on this. Is there a *celebrity* who cares about the polar icecap? Is there a *ribbon*? If there's not a ribbon, move on . . . Arts and Leisure!

DARREN: We have a story on cruise ships.

TINA: That will tie in nicely with the resort-wear coverage . . .

DARREN: It seems they avoid paying taxes by claiming no permanent residence . . .

TINA: *(Interested.)* How do they avoid taxes?

DARREN: And they evade the environmental laws in the same way . . .

TINA: Environmental laws! You're Gore-ing me!

DARREN: They're dumping waste off the Hamptons.

TINA: *(Horrified.)* What!? Where in the Hamptons?

DARREN: The North Fork, I think . . .

TINA: Oh, that's all right then. Haven't you got anything on Diana?

MELISSA: Diana who?

JEREMY: Princess Diana.

TIM: She's dead.

TINA: Perfect! We can make it all up! Look, you're Arts and Leisure, you're not the Green Party. Have you seen this month's *Vogue?* No? It's on the stands people! Now here's a story: *Who shouldn't have waist-length hair? Pastry cooks, women with short necks and anyone over forty unless they're Cher or Madonna!* Now who's on *that?*
(Buzzer buzzes.)

INTERCOM: Margaret Bourke-White to see you.

TINA: As if! How can Madonna and Cher wear their hair long when the rest of us can't? I resent it frankly and I know a lot of our readers do too.

TIM: It just seems like the paper of record . . .

TINA: The paper of record! They go straight to Jane Brody, I promise you. They want to know about their knees. They don't want to know about krill. Write that down, Jeremy, I've learned a new word today. I made a commitment when I took this job to get people to read the front section of this newspaper and I want each and everyone one of you to take responsibility for making that happen.

DARREN: How about a story on Princess Diana's charities? *(No response.)* And . . . her hair?

TINA: I love it! She was very concerned about fashion . . .

DARREN: And land mines.

TINA: Diamond?

TIM: The kind that blows up little children.

TINA: I'm against that. I am firmly against that! Can you get a photo of a child being blown up? No, never mind, forget I said it. People are having breakfast. We'll run a photo of Diana . . . bring in the Diana file, sweet thing . . .

(Jeremy wheels in an entire file cabinet.)

Find a photo where she looks concerned about something other than Camilla . . .

(Jeremy begins to sort through folders. The intercom buzzes.)

INTERCOM: Ben Bradlee on line six.

TINA: Ben Bradlee? Ben Bradlee? Why is that name familiar?

JEREMY: *All the President's Men.*

TINA: He's in the movie?! Buzz him through!

TIM: He wasn't *in* the movie, he was a *character* in the movie . . .

TINA: He's not an actor?

TIM: *No.*

TINA: *(Into intercom.)* Take a message.

JEREMY: Jason Robards played him.

TINA: *(Into intercom.)* Is he still there?

INTERCOM: He's hung up.

TINA: *(Sadly.)* I adore Jason Robards.

MELISSA: Jason Robards is very concerned about the polar ice cap.

TINA: Is he?

MELISSA: He wears a little white ribbon everywhere he goes . . .

TINA: Does he?

MELISSA: You must have noticed . . .

TINA: When you're with Jason Robards, who's looking at ribbons . . . ?

MELISSA: He's adopted three Inuit children . . .

TIM: He vacations in the Honduras . . .

DARREN: He gets there by cruise ship . . .

TINA: Enough! The polar ice cap goes above the fold. We'll run it with a picture of Robards. Below the fold, the blown-up-the-little-children with concerned Diana photo, Tim that's yours, and Darren, put your best reporter on waist-length hair!

(The intercom buzzes.)

INTERCOM: God on line 5.

TINA: Harvey?

INTERCOM: No. God.

TINA: God who?

INTERCOM: Jesus Christ.

JEREMY: *The Greatest Story Ever Told.*

TINA: *Oh.* Try *son* of. Talk about padding your resume. Get a number.

INTERCOM: He's wondering about long hair this spring . . .

TINA: Tell him to watch this space!

END OF PLAY

PLAYS FOR
SIX OR MORE
ACTORS

Toys in Babeland

Delilah Gomez

This play was originally produced as a staged reading at the Queensborough Community College Annual Ten Minute Play Contest in May of 2005. The original cast was as follows: Narrator: Jessica Morgan; Clown: Matthew Dean Wood; Teddy: Michael Aquilino; Panda Bear: Christos Pandelidis; G.I. Joe: Jean-Luc Lodescar Jr.; Dinosaur: John Markisch; Trophy: Manny Blu; Spiderman: Kane Chiang; Stage Manager: Chrislie Francois; Directed by Delilah Gomez. This play was also performed as a staged reading at the American Theatre College Festival in SUNY New Paltz in January of 2006. *Toys In Babeland* was featured in the Fringe Festival and the cast consisted of: Narrator: Diana Lovrin; Clown: Matthew Dean Wood; Teddy: Michael Aquilino; Panda Bear: Paul Ribolotto; G.I. Joe: Tyrell Howard; Dinosaur: Fernando Hernandez; Trophy: Michael Pichardo; Spiderman: Kane Chiang; Stage Manager: Simone Black; Directed by Delilah Gomez.

CHARACTERS

CLOWN

TEDDY

SPIDERMAN

DINOSAUR

TROPHY

G.I. JOE

PANDA

SETTING

Alejandro's room

· · ·

Alejandro's room. An array of toys played by actors are scattered around the room. On the dresser sits a Clown, a tattered Teddy Bear is by the television, and a Panda Bear on the upper corner of the bed by the pillow. G.I. Joe is posed on a shelf with a Dinosaur, a Trophy of a figure of a guy making a basketball shot and a Spiderman action figure. Alejandro is in the bed, and the lights are off. He is with a Girl. Giggles and soft moans from Alejandro and The Girl.

CLOWN: I can't see shit from here. Teddy, you see anything?

TEDDY: Not really. Ever since his kid sister bit my left eye off, I've had some trouble focusing from a distance.

SPIDERMAN: Golly. He must really like this one. He hasn't canned her yet for not putting out and it's been, like, two weeks!

DINOSAUR: Maybe it's love.

SPIDERMAN: What would you know about love, Rex? Any girl that kisses you would have her lips turned into sushi!

DINOSAUR: Mary Jane didn't seem to mind last night!

SPIDERMAN: What'd you say about M.J.?!

DINOSAUR: I said —

TROPHY: Hey, we all have to pose on the same shelf, so why don't you two stop acting like you're still in the toy chest and be a little civil?

CLOWN: Hey-hey! I think I saw a bra just hit the floor!

G.I. JOE: I'll scan the perimeter using my infrared action goggles! Infrared goggles activate!

CLOWN: See anything?

G.I. JOE: Gentlemen, there is confirmation that the unidentified object in question was indeed a brassiere!

(Hurrahs in unison.)

TEDDY: I remember the good old days when I used to be on the bed . . . Now, that dumb-ass panda bear he won at Coney Island is in my place. For all we know, that thing's made out of polyester! It's not even a real bear! He's a purple panda! What bear is purple?!

CLOWN: Leave the bear alone, Teddy. He's having a hard enough time as it is learning English. Last thing he needs is a bitter old sack of fluff like you hassling him. *(To Panda.)* Hey, Panda! You see anything?

PANDA: *(Unsure, but not wanting to be rude. Nods so they'll leave him alone, saying the only English he knows.)* Very good.

TEDDY: *(Pauses, then snickers.)* He don't have a clue. You can say anything to him. Hey, Panda! You want to lick balls?

PANDA: Very good. Yes.

CLOWN: That's fucked up, Teddy. Panda, can you see any action going on over there?

PANDA: *(Apologetically.)* Uh, . . . uh, . . . *Duibuqi. Wo bu dong Yingwen.*

CLOWN: Goddamn, the bear's speakin' Chinese again.

SPIDERMAN: Well, duh! He was made in China!

(Alejandro arises from the bed and goes over to the dresser's top drawer.)

TROPHY: Thank you, Captain Obvious!

TEDDY: Where's he going? Clown, what is he doing?

CLOWN: He's . . . opening the drawer . . . moving all his socks aside . . . he's got something in his hand . . . I can't really see what it is, it's too dark . . . *Joe!*

G.I. JOE: Activating infrared goggles! . . . It's . . . it's . . . Whoa, baby!

SPIDERMAN: What is it, you dumb muscle head ?!

G.I. JOE: I do believe he is retrieving a ribbed, ultra-sensitive protective latex barrier with an expiration date of 2008!

SPIDERMAN: What the hell is that?!

TROPHY: A condom, you web-slinging dolt!

DINOSAUR: Wow, it's about time!

CLOWN: Yeah, two weeks, man.

DINOSAUR: No, I mean that it's about time someone told Spidey exactly what he is!

SPIDERMAN: What!? Listen you prehistoric piece of squeaking plastic! If I had opposable thumbs I'd take you by the tail and —

(Spiderman's voice box goes off.)

"Spidey senses tingling!!" Aw, fuck! Not again! "Spidey senses tingling!"

(Dinosaur is laughing at Spiderman.)

TROPHY: What the hell is wrong with him?

CLOWN: His voice box is on the fritz. Probably got himself too worked up.

SPIDERMAN: "Spidey senses tingling!"

TEDDY: He's been like this ever since the dog got a hold of him
(Alejandro gets up, walks toward the shelf. Alejandro grabs Spiderman and smacks him a couple of times until his voice box stops.)

SPIDERMAN: Ouch! Ooh! Eeh! Ow!! "Spidey senses tingling!" Agh! —
(Spiderman is stuffed under the bed.)
(Alejandro goes back to the bed. Pause.)

CLOWN: He deserved that.

DINOSAUR: Shit, yeah! Remember how he used to say Miss Piggy was a slut 'cause she was always getting fisted?

TROPHY: Yeah. How could she not? *She was a hand puppet!* He used to say that shit just to be an asshole.

TEDDY: I hope he ends up in a yard sale or something . . .
(Pause. The bed begins to squeak.)

PANDA: *(Excitedly.)* Tai hao le! Tai hao le!!

CLOWN: Crap! Seems like Panda's got quite the view!

TEDDY: Do you see anything, Clown?

CLOWN: Just a big lump under the blankets. Gosh. Makes me wish his little sister would choose me to play tea party with. How do you do it, Joe?

G.I. JOE: Well, let's just say that the ladies have a thing for battle scars.

TEDDY: Really? My left eye is missing! You think they'd like that?!

G.I. JOE: That's a Negative. I did not say amputee. *(Beat.)* Did I ever tell you men about last time his little sister took me to play in the tub with her Malibu Barbie?

CLOWN: Aw, don't remind me! I'm still jealous.

G.I. JOE: Heh, heh, heh . . . Did you guys notice that Malibu Barbie set up a nursery in the dream house?

DINOSAUR: Don't tell me you —

TEDDY: You're a dad?!

G.I. JOE: The proud father of a new baby Kelly, complete with thumb-sucking action.

TROPHY: You gonna move in with her, now?

G.I. JOE: Negative. I'm stationed here in Alejandro's room.

CLOWN: Well, Congratulations! Why didn't you tell us sooner?!

G.I. JOE: I wasn't sure until this morning if the little bundle of plastic was mine. Malibu Barbie also took a swim with a Stretch Armstrong and Doctor Ken.

TROPHY: That Doctor Ken, I can only wonder about his bedside manner . . . I think he's honestly been with all of them.

DINOSAUR: Except the Troll! Who'd want to touch that thing? I'd rather get with a Cabbage Patch Kid!

CLOWN: Apparently, you're supposed to rub the gemstone on her belly and make a wish.

DINOSAUR: Maybe she should wish not to be so ugly!

TROPHY: Maybe she should wish that everyone else was uglier. Then she wouldn't look so bad.

CLOWN: We're all ugly, let's face it. My mouth looks like I tried to put lipstick on while in an airplane bathroom, Trophy's forever shooting hoops, Teddy's got no eye, G.I. Joe's hands are bigger than his head, and Panda's fuckin' made of purple polyester.

TROPHY: Well, I'll tell you one thing — it's much better than being able to bleed!

END OF PLAY

at the time . . .

WINTER MILLER

at the time . . . was originally commissioned by the Victory Project, Columbia University.

CHARACTERS

CHARLA

DANA

ELI

ALIZA

AUGUSTUS

STACI

SAMMI

CHAD

SETTING

A classroom

. . .

We are in a classroom. All that's needed to get this across are seven desks, or even chairs, facing front. Somewhere, there's a pencil sharpener.

Students sit at their desks, reading or writing silently.

Dana and Charla are drawing at their desks in charcoal on big white pieces of paper.

CHARLA: What's that?

DANA: I don't know. Looks cool. Life. Strife. Knife.

CHARLA: Wife. So?

DANA: I woke up this morning, first thing ran through my head was: I don't want to die. I don't care if it's in New York City, on the street, in the air, on a mountain, or in my bedroom, I don't want to die.

CHARLA: Not ever?

DANA: Never. Too much I wanna see, too much I wanna do — and it might take me years to figure out who I am and what I'm doing here — say I finally figure that out and boom! It's the end.

CHARLA: You could die old.

DANA: I just don't want to ever. I know I won't be ready.

CHARLA: I could die tomorrow.

DANA: Hey shut up.

CHARLA: I would die a virgin.

DANA: You're gonna jinx yourself.

CHARLA: I said I *could,* not that I would.

DANA: Still bad luck —

CHARLA: All's I said was I could die tomorrow — I'm just not scared of it, like some people.

DANA: Fine. Just shut up about it.

CHARLA: Shut up? Like I can't speak my mind, like you decided it's not a free country?

DANA: What are you, five? *(Baby voice.)* "It's a free country . . ."

CHARLA: Is it a free country or is it not?

(Beat.)

DANA: What's your problem?

CHARLA: Um.

DANA: Seriously.

CHARLA: You got all fascist on me. Oh man you messed me up —

DANA: What's that supposed to be?

CHARLA: Those are his knees. Obviously.

DANA: You think Mikkel's hot?

CHARLA: Are you kidding me? You like him?

DANA: Did I say I did?

CHARLA: He's triple ugly.

DANA: I don't like him.

CHARLA: He's so ugly blind people cross the street.

INTERCOM VOICE-OVER: All teachers please report to the second-floor conference room immediately. Designated students will maintain order, class will continue uninterrupted.

(The students remain in tableau. Eli abruptly puts down his pencil and bursts out of his chair onto his desk and is racing around the room, Matrix style. No one else bats an eye.)

ELI: I want to be extraordinary — as in drop-your-jaw awesome! My relatives and stupid people are always asking me, "What do I want to be when I grow up?" You know what I wanna be? I wanna be a freakin' superhero! No tights. No cape. I'll have six-pack abs and I'll wear all black and I'll take care of whatever needs to be done — some old lady falls down SWOOOOP I catch her. Some idiot tries to put a cap in somebody's ass SWOOOOP I catch the bullet between my teeth, remove it, and smile. Maybe I sock the guy in the stomach, but then I'm up, off, onto the next emergency. I save babies, rescue kittens from trees, change flat tires, and wipe out evil. I deal with the mundane to the highly sensational, I do not discriminate when it comes to crisis. And nine times out of ten, I get the girl. Not ten out of ten. Because there's gotta be some challenge left in life. And when people talk about me, there's not a lot of bullcrap fanfare and hero worship — I don't need to be on the cover of *Newsweek* cause it's just like, yeah, that dude Eli, he's cool, you can depend on him.

(Eli goes back to reading his book and answering quiz questions.)

ALIZA: Jeeeeeeessuuuuuuusss Christ! And I'm not even religious, but good Lord, great Allah, whomever — I CAN'T CONCENTRATE! The Civil War is a vague recollection. The Holocaust — I'm cool, I read Anne Frank, I saw *Schindler's List,* I know enough. The Cuban Missile Crisis — what? The Iran Contra Hearings — does anyone who wasn't alive then really care? I don't need politics and corruption; I need Julian Kipanski. The Persian Gulf War — that was Saddam, right? I cannot stop thinking about this boy!

(Aliza stands up on her chair like she's the missing cousin of the Von Trapps and belts out an ode to true love.)

ALIZA: *(Belts.)* "Hey Julian, do you know I love you,

I need you Julian Kipanski,

I want to kiss you on a jet ski . . .

Hey Julian, you're the reason I'm alive,

I've been in love since we were five.

ALIZA: *(Spoken, yet enthusiastic, and filled with hope.)* I walk up to him, raise my sunglasses really cool and say "Hi, would you like to have dinner with me at an Ethiopian restaurant?" And he smiles and he says, "Aliza, right? Fifth period geometry?" And I say, "Yeah, that's me, but I always sit near the front so I didn't think you'd ever seen my face . . ." and he says, "Of course I did, your face is indelible" — no he would not say indelible — "unforgettable" and I would smile and laugh and he would say, "I would love to have dinner with such a beautiful and intelligent girl" — or would he say woman? "Woman" and then I would say —

(Tableau as:)

INTERCOM VOICE-OVER: All teachers please report to the second-floor conference room immediately. Designated students will maintain order, class will continue uninterrupted.

(Augustus writes in his notebook.)

AUGUSTUS: Tell us about yourself. Who is Augustus Carleton Jones? *(He thinks.)* I'm a guy — I'm seventeen years old, I'm a Leo — but not typically because I don't brag and I don't go on about myself — except when stupid college applications ask me to . . . *(Pause.)* Who am I?

(Big, booming.)

I AM A YOUNG BLACK MAN *(Echo.)* MAN MAN MAN MAN. That's stupid. I AM A BLACK MAN. *(He lets out a giant roar.)* "HIDE YOUR WOMEN, LOCK YOUR CAR, GIVE ME ALL YOUR BASKETBALLS — I AM MR. BLACK MAAAAAAAAAAN! I'M ANGRY — ATHLETIC — I'M A RAPPER, A MUGGER, A THUG, A PLAYAH, A WELFARE-LIVIN' KID, I'M NOTHIN' BUT A

NIGGAH! SO LET ME IN YOUR UNIVERSITY BECAUSE YOU *NEED* MY KIND OF RENAISSANCE MAN!

(Beat.)

Who am I? I'm Augustus Carleton Jones, I'm seventeen years old and I'm trying to figure out who I am. I like words, I'm strong, I work hard, and I'm probably the only kid in this whole school who's got a dad he's never told to his face, "I love you." Can't get the words out. I tried to write 'em, couldn't do that either. But I think if somebody had taught me to say it when I was like six, it would be easy, I'd say it all the time probably. He would pass me the chicken and rice at dinner and I would smile and say, "Ahhh, Dad, I love you, man" and it would be as easy as saying "Can I get some of those green beans too?" Maybe when I get married, he'll look at me and say, "Son, I'm proud of you and I love you." And I'll say it back. Maybe it would be easier if he said it first. Even once. Hey kiddo, I love you.

(Augustus goes back to writing.)

AUGUSTUS: My name is Augustus Carleton Jones and I am a seventeen-year-old black boy from the Bronx. I will be the first in my family to attend college.

(Chad jumps out of his seat, struts down the aisle, runway style, sharpens his pencil. All the students look up and eye him. Chad shrugs his shoulders and glides to his seat. All eyes go back to their papers.)

STACI: *(Reading her exam.)* "In an arithmetic sequence, A = 3 and D = 4. What is the third term in this sequence?" I should tell her he cheated because she thinks he's perfect. I could say he was with some girl from another school. She'd ask me how I know . . . ? I'd say I saw them holding hands and followed them and saw them kissing, but they never saw me. She could tell him she knows he cheated and break up with him. "A one = 3 and D equals" — what if he told her? She didn't call me last night and I didn't see her in homeroom. She's gonna hate me! Why did I do it? I wasn't thinking — I didn't mean to do it. One minute we were talking about her and the next he was kissing me. He kissed me! I just kissed him back. I'm the worst best friend ever.

(She looks at her paper.)

If best friend A fools around with D's boyfriend, use the binomial theorem to calculate the extent to which A's best friend will never speak to her again. I wish I could take it back. Undo it. What's gonna happen when I see them together? What if he didn't tell her and she doesn't know? Maybe she has no idea?

(She looks at her paper.)

"Determine a sequence that has two geometric means between" Staci and

Robbie . . . Maya and Robbie! What's wrong with me? Focus! This is pre-calculus. You know this stuff in your sleep. Easy A. Easy A — I'm the one who's easy — how could I let him kiss me? It's his fault — I didn't ask to be kissed!

(She looks at her paper.)

"Evaluate S to the tenth." What kind of person does this to her best friend? I'll never do it again. Ever. Maybe she won't find out. I'll tell her after they break up. She doesn't need to know right now.

(She looks at her paper.)

"The tenth term is $27.3n = 3n$ over $2x$ because 3 equals —" I'll tell her. I'll apologize and say her friendship means more to me than anything else, that I made a mistake and if she can't forgive me for a moment of bad judgment then I guess we weren't best friends after all. "If $A = 3$ and $D = 4$, then —

INTERCOM VOICE-OVER: All teachers please report to the second-floor conference room immediately. Designated students will maintain order, class will continue uninterrupted.

SAMMI: The thing I think is most important in your life to do is: *(She puts the pen down.)* How can you pick one thing? It's important to love your family. Ah, OK, so what? How does that benefit everyone else? Treat people with respect. *(Pause.)* Is that enough? I guess if you respect someone else's ideas or their beliefs. Yeah. Everybody gets to be who they want to be and they can decide what God they want to worship — if any — they can create their own identity. *(She picks the pen up.)* When you're born, you get a bunch of legos, and you're told to build yourself a personality. *(She looks around the room.)* I'm not better and I'm not worse than the kid next to me. And also — you know what else I was thinking — the Jews are *not* the chosen people. Everybody's chosen, it's up to you to figure out what for. *(She writes.)* This is how I change the world: I don't make judgments, I figure everybody's got a reason. And in some way or another, it's valid.

(Chad interrupts, breaking the tip of his pencil. He rises to sharpen it.)

ALIZA: Why doesn't he use a pen?

ELI: I have a pen, want it?

CHAD: No thanks.

(Chad glides to the sharpener.)

CHAD: I suck at biology. I could give a rat's left nut. When am I gonna use any of this crap? I didn't even study. I tried, but I couldn't stay focused. I got other talents. I called a girl sexy once and I think she liked it because she started smiling and we had a good conversation after. I'm studying in my room last night, I was really trying, and my mom comes in and you know what she does? She asks me this question out of nowhere. She says, "Are you gay?" Am I gay? I was like, Mom, "Do you know how many girls want to go out with me? I could get any girl I want. If I wanted to be with a guy then I guess I would, cause I don't care what people think." She said, "You *would be* with another guy or you *have been* with another guy?" This was outta nowhere — I was like — No, Mom, I haven't, because I'm not interested. You know what she said? I kid you not, this is what she said: "If you haven't tried it, then how do you know you don't like it?" Like being with a guy is like having Brussels sprouts? I said, I don't know Mom, I'll be sure to ponder that supposition, but right now I gotta lot of homework, and I got a bio test tomorrow. All she said was, "Don't fail this one." And shut the door. Why would I want to hook up with another guy? We both got fire hoses, so what would we get out of it? I'm gonna fail this test. I got too much on my mind to think about biology.

INTERCOM VOICE-OVER: All teachers please report to the second-floor conference room immediately. Designated students will maintain order, class will continue uninterrupted.

ALL IN UNISON: I remember exactly where I was when I found out.

DANA: I was in art class with Charla.

CHARLA: I was wearing my Lucky jeans.

CHAD: I was failing a biology test.

ALL IN UNISON: The teacher came in and said:

AUGUSTUS: I want you to remain calm.

ALIZA: I have some horrible news to share.

ELI: This morning, at 8:46 A.M.

ALL IN UNISON: First one airplane and then another —

SAMMI: My first thought was, let's kill whoever did this.

ELI: I'm not a superhero.

AUGUSTUS: If there's a draft, black men like me will be the first to die.

STACI: I'm sorry for everything I ever did that hurt someone else.

ALIZA: I don't know if I believe in God. And if I didn't five minutes ago, why would I believe now? And if I did five minutes ago, why would I believe now?

CHAD: The test isn't going to matter five minutes from now.

CHARLA: I'm telling you, you never know when you're gonna die.

DANA: I don't wanna die, I don't care if it's in New York City, in the street, in the air, on a mountain, or in my bedroom, I don't want to die.

END OF PLAY

Small World

TRACEY SCOTT WILSON

CHARACTERS
    MAN
    WOMAN
    MAN 2
    WOMAN 2
    MAN 3
    WOMAN 3

SETTING
    Three benches

• • •

Lights up on six couples meeting at separate benches. They have never met before. It is a first date for all. Until specified, Man 1 speaks only to Woman 1. Man 2 only speaks to Woman 2 and Man 3 only speaks to Woman 3. When it reads. Man 1, 2, etc. . . . the characters are speaking simultaneously. Also (. . .) indicates that the characters are finishing the previous sentence.

MAN 1: Stacy?

WOMAN 1: Bob?

MAN 2: Lucy?

WOMAN 2: Bill?

MAN 3: Alice?

WOMAN 3: Tim?

ALL: Hi!

MAN 1: I've never been on one of these blind . . .

MAN 2: . . . Computer..

MAN 3: . . . newspaper ad . . .

MAN 1, 2, 3: Dates before.

WOMAN 1, 2, 3: Neither have I.
    (They sit.)

MEN 1, 2: It's beautiful here in the park.

MAN 3: Maybe we should have gone to the park.

WOMAN 1, 2: Yes.

WOMAN 3: No.

MAN 3: Oh.

WOMAN 3: I have allergies. *(Pause.)* But still you . . .

WOMAN 1, 2, 3: . . . couldn't ask for a more . . .

WOMAN 1: Beautiful . . .

WOMAN 2: Wonderful . . .

WOMAN 3: Pretty . . .

WOMAN 1, 2, 3: day today.

MAN 1, 2: Would you like to go for a walk around the . . . .

MAN 1: Lake.

MAN 2: Flower garden.

MAN 3: Wanna go to a movie?

WOMAN 1: Maybe in a minute.

WOMAN 2: I'd like to sit here for a few minutes.

WOMAN 3: Can we talk first?

MAN 1, 2, 3: OK.

ALL: So . . .

WOMAN 1, 2: I understand you work in . . .

WOMAN 1: . . . the health care . . .

WOMAN 2: . . . the music . . .

WOMAN 1, 2: industry.

WOMAN 3: I am so lonely.

MAN 1: Yes, I am a home health aid for the elderly.

MAN 2: Yes, I'm writing a book on jazz.

MAN 3: I . . . uh . . .

WOMAN 1, 2: That's . . .

WOMAN 1: Wonderful.

WOMAN 2: Exciting.

WOMAN 3: Please help me.

MAN 1, 2: So . . .

MAN 3: Uh . . .

MAN 1, 2: What do you do?

MAN 3: How can I help you?

WOMAN 1: Oh, I'm just an office manager for a small office.

WOMAN 2: I'm a computer consultant.

WOMAN 3: Just be real with me.

WOMAN 1, 2: But I really want to . . .

WOMAN 3: Be really, really, really, really, really real with me.

WOMAN 1: . . . work in TV.

WOMAN 2: . . . own a farm someday.

WOMAN 3: Un-orchestrate your emotions to my song.

MAN 1: Interesting.

MAN 2: Great.

MAN 3: Wait a minute.

MAN 1: I have a friend . . .

MAN 2: I know someone . . .

MAN 3: Have you read that book . . . ?

MAN 1: Works in TV.

MAN 2: Who owns a farm.

MAN 3: *(Recalling title of book.)* Think It . . .

WOMAN 3: Say It . . .

MAN 3: Speak It . . .

MAN 3/WOMAN 3: Now! *The Interactive Guide to Kicking Your Inner-Child's Ass.*

MAN 1: She says TV is . . .

MAN 2: He says farming is . . .

MAN 3: I love that book.

MAN 1, 2: a lot of work.

MAN 3: It changed my life.

MAN 1, 2 : . . . but rewarding.

WOMAN 1: Yeah.

WOMAN 2: Yup.

WOMAN 3: It changed my life too. *(Pause.)* Before I read that book I was so polite all the time. I was into . . .

WOMAN 3/MAN 3: Pseudo-Ultra-Judo-Fake Bonding.

WOMAN 3: Like it says in the book! I would have met you here today and just had a . . .

WOMAN 1, 2: So . . .

WOMAN 3: Shallow conversation . . .

WOMAN 1, 2: It must be really rewarding to . . .

WOMAN 3: . . . about nothing.

WOMAN 1: . . . help the elderly . . .

WOMAN 2: . . . write about jazz.

WOMAN 3: But because of that book I feel strong enough to say to you: HELP ME!

MAN 1, 2: It's so rewarding.

MAN 1: I couldn't even begin to tell you.

MAN 2: Jazz is my life.

MAN 3: I will help you. What's wrong?

WOMAN 3: You see I'm not really over my . . .

> *(Lights up on Man 1.)*

WOMAN 3: . . . last boyfriend.

MAN 1: *(To Woman 1.)* Some people get depressed when they look at the elderly.

WOMAN 3: He told me he was a home health aid for the elderly.

MAN 1: *(To Woman 1.)* But I don't. I feel hopeful . . .

WOMAN 3: But he only had one patient.

MAN 1: . . . to have lived so long and experienced so much.

WOMAN 3: . . . his mother.

MAN 1: *(To Woman 1.)* It's a beautiful thing.

WOMAN 1: *(To Man 1.)* Wow . . .

MAN 3: Ewwwww.

WOMAN 3: Every time I would go over his house he would excuse himself every few minutes, and go into another room. I just thought he had a bladder problem, but then one day I heard someone talking. I asked him *(To Man 1.)* who was that? . . .

MAN 1: *(To Woman 3.)* No one. You're hearing things. I live alone.

WOMAN 3: *(To Man 3.)* But one day, I tiptoed behind him and peeked in the room. There was an old woman in a chair. He was calling her . . .

MAN 1: Momma.

WOMAN 3: *(To Man 3.)* I was very understanding. *(To Man 1.)* Oh, honey. Is this your mother? You take care of her too? That's nothing to be ashamed of. It's sweet. Your mother and all those others too. *(To Man 3.)* Then this woman, who is like so wrinkled a prune would stare in awe, says . . .

WOMAN 2: *(As mother.)* Who are you! Who are you! I'm his one and only patient! His one and only! Get Out! I'm the only one who gets their feet shaved around here. You're stepping on my toenail clippings! GET OUT! GET OUT!

WOMAN 3: Two days later he was like:

MAN 1: *(To Woman 3.)* I tried to be a home health worker, but Momma takes up all of my time. I love Momma, I love Momma, I love Momma. I do. Before that she and Grandma took up all of my time. I love Grandma, I love Grandma, I love Grandma. I do. But Grandma is dead now, and soon . . . Momma will be dead too. Then you can move into my house, and we'll have kids. Two boys and two girls. We'll teach them to be good little home health workers too, cause, like Momma says, by the time we grow old our Social Security check won't buy us a cup of milk.

WOMAN 1: *(To Man 1)* You are so noble.

MAN 3: Ew.

WOMAN 3: But still I think of him.

MAN 3: I know what you mean. I'm still hung up on my girlfriend too. *(Lights up on Woman #2.)*

MAN 3: She said she wanted to be a farmer.

WOMAN 2: *(To Man 2.)* I know it's a lot of work, but to be out in the fresh country air . . .

MAN 3: . . . a chicken farmer.

WOMAN 2: *(To Man 2.)* Communing with nature every day. Feeding the land. Feeding the chickens.

MAN 3: But that not all she wanted to do with those chickens.

(Man 3 squirms in his chair.)

WOMAN 2: *(To Man 3.)* What' wrong with you?

MAN 3: I've got hay in my butt. God, that is the last time we go to a farm.

WOMAN 2: What? No!

MAN 3: Yes, it is.

WOMAN 2: But farming is my life.

MAN 3: But you don't own a farm, I don't understand why we have to sneak in other people's barns to make love all the time. At first, it was exciting, but now it's just weird.

WOMAN 2: You're so conventional.

MAN 3: I am not . . . I . . .

(There is the sound of a chicken.)

MAN 3: What was that?

(Sound of a chicken.)

WOMAN 2: Nothing.

MAN 3: Yes, it was.

(Sound of a chicken.)

MAN 3: It sounded like . . . *(To Woman 3.)* I opened the door and there were all these chickens. Chickens everywhere.

MAN 2: What the . . .

WOMAN 2: Don't touch them. I love them. See how soft and gentle.

MAN 2: You can't . . . We can't keep chickens in the apartment.

WOMAN 2: Quiet. Don't yell in front of them. *(Pause.)* See they are sweet and gentle. Like kittens with feathers. But sexy. Very sexy. That clucking drives me wild. Please just touch the chickens' baby! Touch the chickens!

MAN 2: *(To Woman 2)* I love nature too.

WOMAN 3: *(To Man 3.)* Yuuccch.

MAN 3: What is wrong with us?

WOMAN 3: For me it has been a pattern. A pattern of unhealthy relationships. The other guy I dated.

(Light up on Man 2.)

WOMAN 3: A die-hard jazz lover.

MAN 2: *(To Woman 2.)* Jazz is truly the only great American art form.

WOMAN 3: So I thought.

MAN 2: In its rhythms we hear America. In its tunes we see ourselves.

WOMAN 3: I studied everything I could about jazz just so I could get close to him. I bought thousands of recordings. One day I bought him this rare Miles Davis recording. It took me six months to find it. I was going to surprise him and slip in his record collection. I must have hit some secret door because . . . *(To Man 2.)* Honey . . .

MAN 2: Yeah, baby.

WOMAN 3: Uh . . . I wanted to give you this. *(Hands him CD.)*

MAN 2: Oh wow. Miles Davis session number 73. Oh wow baby, thank you, thank you.

WOMAN 3: Uh-huh. Um . . . I was going put it in with your other records . . . and surprise you.

MAN 2: Uh-huh. This is perfect.

WOMAN 3: And I found this.

(Woman shows him CD.)

MAN 2: Oh . . . Uh . . . Yeah, you know. I was holding that for my . . . mother. My mother. .

WOMAN 3: *(To Man 3.)* A Yanni CD.

WOMAN 3: *(To Man 2.)* No, you weren't.

(She dumps a whole batch of CDs at his feet.)

WOMAN 3: Yanni, John Tesh, Enya, Celine Dion, Phil Collins . . . What is this about? I thought you were cool.

MAN 2: Hey! Be careful. You're going to scratch them. *(Pause.)* One night I couldn't sleep, alright. So, I turned on the radio. They were playing "Desert Siren" by Yanni. *(He hums tune.)* It was so relaxing. *(He hums tune.)* So calming. *(He hums tune.)* Yanni is beautiful *(He hums tune.)* Someday he'll be appreciated. *(He hums tune.)* Someday . . . *(He hums.)* Someday.

WOMAN 2: *(To Man 2.)* I want you to teach me everything you know about music.

MAN 3: *(Shudders.)* John Tesh. Ewww.

WOMAN 3: So, you see. It must be me.

MAN 3: No, no, no. Don't assume that. I dated this woman.

WOMAN 1: *(To Man 1.)* I know TV is supposed to be this vast wasteland.

MAN 3: Who wanted to work in TV

WOMAN 1: *(To Man 1.)* But I think it is a powerful and effective medium . . .

MAN 3: So, she watched a lot of TV.

WOMAN 1: *(To Man 1.)* — to communicate and express ideas.

MAN 3: But then I noticed she began to watch only one program.

(Theme from The Jeffersons *plays.)*

MAN 3: *(To Woman 1.)* Honey, do we have to watch . . .

WOMAN 1: Shhhhh.

MAN 3: But you've seen this episode a hundred times already.

WOMAN 1: Shhhhh.

MAN 3: All day and night, *The Jeffersons.* She would tape the show watch it in fast forward and reverse.

WOMAN 1: *(Pointing to TV.)* See! Right there! Right there!

MAN 3: What?

WOMAN 1: Lionel just said . . . Pop Taht Tuoba Erus Ton Mi

MAN 3: What?

WOMAN 1: He said: Pop Taht Tuoba Erus Ton Mi

MAN 3: What? What are you saying?

WOMAN 1: Oh, I have a little language for Lionel. You see, I believe he's giving me a message , so I speak his lines backwards so I can understand.

MAN 3: Giving you a message?

WOMAN 1: Yes. Us. Us a message. To the world.

MAN 3: Uh . . .

WOMAN 1: Did you know Lionel created the show *Good Times.* . . .

MAN 3: Uh . . . Honey.

WOMAN 1: And the man that replaced him on the show was his brother. His very own brother.

MAN 3: Honey, I . . .

WOMAN 1: But he's gone now. No word of him since 1979. I can't find him. But I will. I know I will. Pop Taht Tuoba Erus Ton Mi Pop. Taht Tuoba Erus Ton Mi Pop. Taht Tuoba Erus Ton Mi

MAN 1: *(To Woman 1.)* I've never thought of TV that way before.

WOMAN 3: *(To Man 3.)* I'll never watch *The Jeffersons* again. *(Pause.)* In honor of you.

MAN 3: Listen, I have to tell you . . .

MAN 1, 2, 3: I really like you.

MAN 1: You're wonderful . . .

MAN 2: . . . .terrific . . .

MAN 3: You've touched my inner song and let me tell you baby, it ain't playing Yanni.

(Girls smile and laugh in unison.)

WOMAN 1, 2, 3: Well . . .

WOMAN 1: I think you're great . . .

WOMAN 2: Fantastic . . .

WOMAN 3: You've touch my inner song . . .

WOMAN 1, 2, 3: . . . too.

MAN 1, 2, 3: I would love to . . .

MAN 1: Get to know you.

MAN 2: Spend some more time with you.

MAN 3: Coordinate your soul with mine.

WOMAN 1, 2, 3: *(They all sigh.)* Great!

MAN 1, 2: But first I have to . . .

MAN 1: Stop at home for a minute.

MAN 2: Stop by the record store.

MAN 3: My afternoon is completely free.

WOMAN 1: Oh, I suppose you have to check on your patients?

WOMAN 2: Are you buying the latest jazz CD?

MAN 1, 2: Uh . . . Yeah . . . Yeah . . .

WOMAN 1, 2: Oh, that works out because I have to . . .

WOMAN 1: Set my VCR to record a program.

WOMAN 2: Stop by this new chicken farm.

WOMAN 3: My afternoon is free too.

WOMAN 1, 2/MAN 1, 2: So, I'll meet you later then.

ALL: Great!

WOMAN 1, 2, 3: But I tell you, I just can't believe someone like you . . .

WOMAN 1: . . . .isn't taken . . .

WOMAN 2: . . . hasn't been snatched up yet . . .

WOMAN 3: . . . is free . . .

MAN 1, 2, 3: Well, I can't believe you are . . .

MAN 1: . . . available . . .

MAN 2: . . . not married . . .

MAN 3: . . . unattached.

ALL: There are just so many crazy people out there.
     (They all laugh.)

WOMAN 1: I'm telling you . . .

MAN 1: You got that right.

WOMAN 2: Tell me about it . . .

MAN 2: I could tell you stories.

WOMAN 3: Hell, between the two of us . . .

MAN 3: I guess we dated every crazy person out there.

WOMAN 1, 2: My last boyfriend . . .

MAN 1, 2: . . . girlfriend . . .
     (Lights up on Man 3 and Woman 3.)

MAN 1, 2/WOMAN 1, 2: was a pathological liar!
     (They gasp in disbelief.)

WOMAN 1: Really?

MAN 1: No kidding.

WOMAN 2: What are the chances of that?

MAN 2: It really is a small world. *(Pause.)* A small world.

END OF PLAY

AUG 29 2007